PERU ESSENTIAL TRAVEL GUIDE BOOK
2024

Victor Smith

Table of Contents

Chapter 1: Introduction to Peru

1.1 Overview of Peru

Peru, a nation in western South America, is well-known for its rich cultural history, diversified landscapes, and historical importance. Bordered by Ecuador and Colombia to the north, Brazil to the east, Bolivia to the southeast, Chile to the south, and the Pacific Ocean to the west, Peru has a geographical variety that includes coastal deserts, Andean mountains, and Amazonian rainforests.

Historical and Cultural Significance

Peru is the core of the Inca kingdom, the most prominent in pre-Columbian America. The Inca civilization, noted for its complex farming practices, architectural wonders, and extensive transportation networks, had a lasting impact on the nation. Machu Picchu, the renowned Inca fortress in the Andes Mountains, is a UNESCO World Heritage Site and one of the World's New Seven Wonders. In addition to the Incas, Peru's history contains influences from previous civilizations, including the Norte Chico, Moche, and Nazca cultures, each adding distinct pieces to Peru's archeological and cultural fabric.

Geography and Climate

Peru's landscape is very diverse, including three separate regions:

The Costa (Coast) is a thin, arid region along the Pacific Ocean that includes significant towns such as Lima, the capital.

The Sierra (Highlands) is the Andean Mountain range, with peaks exceeding 6,000 meters and high-altitude communities like Cusco and Arequipa.

The Selva (Jungle) refers to the immense Amazon rainforest, rich in biodiversity and indigenous cultures.
Peru's climate varies substantially by area. The coastline has moderate, arid weather, while the highlands have a temperate climate with dry and rainy seasons. The rainforest area is distinguished by a hot, humid environment with heavy yearly rains.

Population & Languages

Peru's population exceeds 33 million, and it is a combination of indigenous peoples, mestizos (people of mixed indigenous and European origin), and European, African, and Asian ancestors. Spanish is the official language spoken by the vast majority of the people. However, indigenous languages like Quechua and Aymara are widely spoken, especially in the highlands.

Economy & Industry

Peru's economy is one of the fastest expanding in South America, thanks to various industries, including mining, agriculture, fishing, and tourism. The nation is among the world's top gold, silver, copper, and zinc producers. The lush valleys of the Andes produce crops such as potatoes, maize, and quinoa, while the coastal seas are teeming with marine life, supporting a vibrant fishing sector.

Tourism is integral to Peru's economy, with people traveling to see its historical monuments, natural beauty, and lively culture. The top tourist sites are Machu Picchu, the Sacred Valley, the Nazca Lines, Lake Titicaca, and the Amazon rainforest.

Cultural Heritage and Traditions

Peruvian culture is a diverse collection of customs shaped by indigenous history, Spanish colonialism, and other immigrant cultures. Festivals are an essential part of Peruvian society, with vivid events such as Inti Raymi (Festival of the Sun), Semana Santa (Holy Week), and the Feast of Corpus Christi drawing both residents and visitors. Traditional music and dance, such as Andean panpipes and the energetic rhythms of marinara and huayno, are essential to the cultural environment.

Peruvian cuisine is known for its variety and taste, which combines indigenous ingredients with culinary influences from throughout the globe. Ceviche (marinated raw seafood), Lomo salt ado (stir-fried beef), and cuy (guinea pig), Peru's emblematic meal, are among its signature foods.

Biodiversity and Natural Wonders

Peru has hundreds of plants, animal, and bird species, making it one of the world's most biodiverse nations. The Amazon rainforest, which spans more than 60% of the nation, is a biodiversity hotspot, home to jaguars, macaws, and pink river dolphins. The Andes include distinctive flora and wildlife, including the Andean condor and the vicuña, a wild progenitor of the alpaca.

To summarize, Peru is a country of contrasts and variety, with a riveting combination of ancient history, cultural richness, and natural beauty. Whether seeing the relics of ancient civilizations, hiking through spectacular landscapes, or experiencing the colorful local culture, Peru offers many educational and adventurous experiences.

1.2 Planning your Trip to Peru

Numerous elements must be carefully considered while planning a vacation to Peru to guarantee a seamless and pleasurable experience. This thorough guide will help you plan your Peruvian journey, from identifying the ideal time to travel and comprehending visa requirements to preparing for the unique climate and cultural subtleties.

The best time to visit

Peru's climate differs dramatically between its three major regions: the coast, the highlands, and the Amazon rainforest. Understanding the optimal time to visit each place is critical for getting the most out of your vacation.

The coastal area, which includes Lima and the northern beaches, is best visited during the Southern Hemisphere summer (December to March) when the weather is pleasant and sunny. However, Lima may be cloudy and cold during winter (June to September).

Highlands: The highland areas, including Cusco and the Sacred Valley, undergo two primary seasons: the dry season (April to October) and the rainy season (November to March). The dry season is suitable for hiking and viewing ancient sites, with clear skies and mild temperatures. Although less busy, the rainy season may bring heavy rain and muddy routes.

Amazon: The jungle is hot and humid all year round. The dry season (May to October) is considered the greatest time to visit since there are fewer insects and lower water levels, making it easier to view animals. The wet season (November to April) provides lush landscapes and high river levels, allowing for deeper jungle adventures by boat.

Visa and Entry Requirements

Peruvian visa requirements differ based on your nationality. Citizens of numerous countries, including the United States, Canada, the European Union, Australia, and New Zealand, do not need a visa for visits of up to 90 days. However, before flying, verify the particular criteria for your nationality.

Passport Validity: Ensure your passport is valid for at least six months beyond your planned stay.

Tourist Visa: Visitors may often be acquired via Peruvian consulates or embassies in your native country. Entry Card: Upon arrival, you will be given an Andean Migration Card (TAM), which you must keep and show upon leaving.

Health & Safety

Take the following health measures to guarantee a safe and healthy vacation to Peru.

Routine vaccines should be kept up to date. Depending on the places you want to travel, you may need additional vaccines for hepatitis A and B, typhoid, and yellow fever.

Altitude Sickness: Altitude sickness may be a worry in high-altitude places like Cusco and Puno. To avoid symptoms, gradually acclimate, remain hydrated, and consider taking acetazolamide.

Mosquito Protection: To avoid mosquito-borne illnesses such as malaria and dengue fever in the Amazon and other lowland regions, apply insect repellent, wear long sleeves and trousers, and sleep beneath mosquito nets.

Travel Insurance: Purchase comprehensive travel insurance that covers medical emergencies, trip cancellations, and theft.

Transportation

Getting through Peru may be an experience in and of itself, with various transportation alternatives.
Domestic flights are the quickest way to travel great distances, with multiple airlines operating flights between major cities and tourist locations.

Buses: Peru has a large bus network that offers luxury buses and more basic alternatives. Companies such as Cruz del Sur and Oltursa provide pleasant long-distance travel.

Train travel is restricted yet picturesque, especially on Peru Rail and Inca Rail's routes to Machu Picchu and Lake Titicaca.

Taxis and ride-sharing: Taxis are readily accessible in cities. Choose recognized providers or applications such as Uber to ensure a safe journey.

Public transportation: Buses and combis (minibuses) are prevalent in cities. However, they need to be more modern and reliable.

Accommodation

Peru has a broad choice of hotel alternatives to fit any budget or desire.

Hotels and Hostels: From luxury hotels and boutique accommodations to low-cost hostels and guesthouses, there is something for everyone.

Eco-Lodges: In the Amazon, eco-lodges provide immersive rainforest experiences while promoting sustainable practices.

Homestays: For a cultural experience, try staying in a homestay, especially in remote places like the Sacred Valley or Lake Titicaca.

Packing Essentials

Packing adequately for Peru's many temperatures and activities is critical.
Layered clothes are essential—lightweight, breathable materials for the coast and jungle, with warmer mountain layers. Remember your rain gear during the rainy season. Footwear includes comfortable walking shoes for city excursions, durable hiking boots for treks, and sandals for beach or resort visits.

Accessories: A decent quality daypack, a wide-brimmed hat, sunglasses, and sunscreen are must-haves.
Trip papers include a passport, copies of critical documents, trip insurance, and an itinerary.
Cultural Considerations
Understanding and respecting local customs and traditions might improve your overall travel experience.

Language: Learning simple Spanish phrases may be helpful. Quechua phrases are popular in highland areas.
Etiquette: Always greet them with a cordial "buenos días" or "buenas tardes." Always get permission before snapping images of them.

Tipping is usual in restaurants (about 10%), and modest amounts are accepted for guides and hotel workers.

By considering these aspects and adequately organizing your trip to Peru, you can guarantee that you will be well-prepared and enjoy the country's numerous beauties and experiences.

1.3 Important Information: Visas, Currency, and Health Precautions

When planning a vacation to Peru, it is essential to be knowledgeable about visas, currencies, and health measures to ensure a smooth and pleasurable visit. Here's a full outline to help you plan.

Visas

Visa Requirements:

Tourist Visa: Citizens of numerous countries, including the United States, Canada, the European Union, Australia, and New Zealand, do not need a visa for tourist stays up to 90 days. However, examining the exact criteria depending on your nationality before flying is essential since they may change.

Extended Stays: If you want to remain for more than 90 days, you may petition for an extension at Peru's Immigration Office. It is suggested that you do this long before your first visa expires.

Business and Other Visas: Different visa requirements apply when going for business, employment, or study, and you must apply for the appropriate visa at a Peruvian consulate or embassy in your home country.

Entry Requirements:

Passport Validity: Ensure your passport is valid for at least six months beyond your planned stay.
Andean Migration Card (TAM): Upon arrival, you will obtain an Andean Migration Card, which you must preserve and submit upon leaving. Losing this card might result in penalties or delays while exiting the country.

Currency
Currency Basics:

Peruvian Sol (PEN): The official currency is the Peruvian Sol, abbreviated as PEN. Carrying some local cash for modest transactions is good since not all places take credit cards.

Currency Rates: Currency rates vary, so verify current rates before exchanging money. Exchange services are offered at airports, banks, and authorized exchange offices (casas de cambio).

Using Money in Peru

ATMs are widely accessible in cities and tourist locations. Most ATMs accept major foreign credit and debit cards; however, some may levy withdrawal fees.

Credit Cards: Accepted at most hotels, restaurants, and stores in metropolitan areas. However, smaller establishments and those in remote locations may only take cash.

Tipping is typical in restaurants (about 10%), and modest gratuities to guides, drivers, and hotel workers are welcomed.

Safety Tips:

Counterfeit Currency: Be wary of counterfeit money. Learn to detect the security features of Peruvian Sol banknotes and only exchange money at recognized locations.

Avoid carrying significant quantities of cash. Use a money belt or concealed bag to safeguard your money and vital papers.

Health precautions

Vaccinations:
Standard immunizations: Make sure you are up to date on standard immunizations, including MMR (measles, mumps, rubella), DTP (diphtheria, tetanus, pertussis), varicella (chickenpox), polio, and flu.

Recommended Vaccinations: Travelers should be vaccinated against hepatitis A and B, typhoid, and yellow fever, mainly if they visit rural or forest regions. Yellow fever immunization is especially advised for anyone traveling the Amazon Basin.

Altitude Sickness:

High-Altitude Areas: Cusco, Puno, and the Sacred Valley are at high elevations. Symptoms of altitude sickness include headaches, nausea, dizziness, and shortness of breath.
To help prevent symptoms, acclimate gradually, remain hydrated, avoid alcohol, and consider taking drugs like acetazolamide.

Treatment: If symptoms linger, rest and, if feasible, reduce your altitude. Seek medical attention if the symptoms are severe.
Water and Food Safety:

Drinking Water: Tap water in Peru is unsafe to consume. When drinking and brushing your teeth, always use bottled or boiling water.

Food Precautions: Eat at recognized restaurants, avoid street food, and ensure the meal is well cooked. Peel or wash fruits and vegetables in filtered water.

Mosquito-borne diseases:

Malaria and dengue fever are present in the Amazon area. Use DEET-based insect repellent, wear long sleeves and trousers, and sleep beneath mosquito netting.

Vaccinations: While there is no vaccination for dengue, following preventative steps may lower the risk. If you plan to travel to high-risk locations, see your doctor about antimalarial drugs.

Travel insurance:

Comprehensive Coverage: Purchase travel insurance that covers medical emergencies, trip cancellations, lost baggage, and theft.

Medical Facilities: Although big cities have excellent medical facilities, rural and isolated places may have restricted access. Make sure your insurance covers medical evacuation if required.

Understanding these practical factors allows you to better prepare for your trip to Peru, resulting in a safer and more pleasurable experience.

1.4 When to Visit: Seasons and Weather

Peru's landforms are varied, with each having its unique climatic patterns. Understanding the seasons and weather is critical for determining the optimum time to visit different places, whether visiting the coastal deserts, the Andean highlands, or the Amazon jungle. Here's a complete guide about when to visit Peru based on the country's several climate zones.

Coastal Region

Geography:

Peru's coastline zone runs along the Pacific Ocean, including essential towns such as Lima and Trujillo and the northern beaches.

Seasons:

Summer (December–March) is the most outstanding season for exploring the seaside area. The weather is pleasant and bright, with temperatures ranging from 25°C to 30°C (77°F to 86°F). This is great for beach sports and discovering coastal sites.

Winter (June to September): The coast has colder temperatures ranging from 15°C to 20°C (59°F to 68°F) and frequent fog, particularly around Lima. While it is still feasible to visit, the weather may not be ideal for outdoor activities.

Best time to visit:
December to March: Ideal for beachgoers and those wishing to explore coastal towns in their prime weather.

Highland Region

Geography:
The highlands, or Sierra, contain the Andean Mountain range and feature renowned tourist locations such as Cusco, the Sacred Valley, Machu Picchu, and Lake Titicaca.

Seasons:

Dry Season (April to October): This is the busiest tourist season, especially for hiking and outdoor activities. The days are mainly bright and dry, with temperatures ranging from 15°C to 20°C (59°F to 68°F). Nights may be chilly, particularly at higher elevations.

Wet Season (November to March): Frequent rain showers may generate muddy routes and landslides, making hiking more difficult. Temperatures are significantly warmer during the day but might remain cold at night.

Best time to visit:
April to October is ideal for hiking the Inca Trail, experiencing Machu Picchu, and visiting highland towns such as Cusco and Arequipa. Clear skies provide breathtaking vistas and ideal circumstances for outdoor activities.

June to August is the most significant tourist season, coinciding with summer holidays in the Northern Hemisphere. You are advised to book your lodgings and trips in advance.

Amazon Rainforest

Geography:
The Amazon rainforest encompasses a large area of eastern Peru, including popular sites such as Iquitos, Puerto Maldonado, and Manu National Park.
Seasons:
The most significant time to visit the Amazon is during the dry season, which runs from May to October. Lower

water levels make routes more accessible and animal viewing easier. The temperature ranges from 25°C to 30°C (77°F to 86°F), with fewer insects.

Wet Season (November to April): The rainforest receives considerable rainfall, high humidity, and average temperatures of 30°C (86°F). Rivers surge, allowing for deeper boat expeditions, although pathways may get inundated, making animals more challenging to observe.

Best time to visit:
May to October is the best time for animal watching, jungle trekking, and rainforest exploration, as fewer mosquitoes and more bearable weather conditions exist.

November to April: Travel is still feasible, but expect rain and high humidity. This season provides beautiful views and a more immersive rainforest experience, although certain activities may be restricted.

Overall, the best time to visit Peru

High Season: June to August is the peak tourist season, particularly in the highlands. It is ideal for hiking and visiting major destinations such as Machu Picchu. However, expect a more excellent crowd and higher pricing.

Shoulder Seasons: April to May and September to October are ideal for beautiful weather and fewer visitors. It's an excellent time to explore all areas of Peru, with more availability and somewhat reduced pricing.

Low season: The best time to explore the coastal regions and the Amazon jungle is from November to March. The highlands may be damp, but if you are okay with rain, you'll find fewer visitors and perhaps cheaper prices.

Understanding seasonal weather patterns throughout Peru's regions allows you to arrange your vacation around the ideal circumstances for your selected activities and attractions. Whether you want to hike historic routes, discover bustling towns, or immerse yourself in the gorgeous Amazon, Peru has an experience for everyone.

1.5 Transportation: Moving Around Peru

Traveling across Peru is an experience, with various transportation alternatives to suit all budgets and inclinations. From contemporary domestic planes and gorgeous train excursions to large bus networks and local taxis, this guide will help you explore the country's many landscapes and towns.

Domestic flights
LATAM Airlines, Avianca, Sky Airline, and Viva Air are the leading airlines that provide domestic flights.
Lima flies to essential towns and tourist attractions like Cusco, Arequipa, Iquitos, Puerto Maldonado, and Juliaca (for Lake Titicaca).

Booking: It is best to book flights in advance, particularly during busy tourist seasons (June to August and December to January).

Advantages
Time-saving: Flights are the quickest way to travel vast distances, like Lima to Cusco or Lima to Iquitos.

Comfort: Modern aircraft with typical facilities provide a pleasant flight.

Tips: Early booking ensures better rates and availability.

Luggage Policies: Check your airline's policy since budget airlines may have stringent limitations and extra surcharges.

Buses
Top bus companies include Cruz del Sur, Oltursa, Civa, and Ormeño. They provide a variety of classes, from economical to luxury.

Routes: Buses operate a vast network, linking cities, towns, and rural regions nationwide.

Comfort: Luxury buses have reclining seats, onboard entertainment, refreshments, and Wi-Fi to make lengthy rides more pleasant.

Advantages
Cost-effective: Buses are often the cheapest option to travel vast distances.

Scenic Routes: Overland travel lets you see Peru's landscapes up close.

Tips: Choose reputed bus companies to ensure your safety and dependability.

Booking: Purchase tickets in advance for popular routes, particularly during holidays and high seasons.

Overnight Buses: To save money on hotels, consider using overnight buses for lengthy excursions.

Trains

The most noteworthy rail lines are Cusco to Machu Picchu (run by Peru Rail and Inca Rail) and the luxury Andean Explorer train from Cusco to Puno (Lake Titicaca) and Arequipa.

Booking: Tickets for popular routes, particularly to Machu Picchu, should be reserved well in advance.

Advantages

Scenic Journeys: Trains provide stunning vistas of the Andes and a unique travel experience.
Comfort and Luxury: Trains like the Belmond Andean Explorer provide a high-end travel experience, including gourmet meals and sumptuous rooms.

Tips

Advance Planning: Book your tickets as soon as possible, especially for popular routes to Machu Picchu.

Travel Class: Select the service level best suits your budget and comfort needs.

Taxis and Ridesharing
Availability: Taxis are widely accessible in cities and towns. Uber, Cabify, and Beat provide ridesharing services in major cities such as Lima and Cusco.

Negotiation: Taxi costs are often adjustable, so settling on a price before beginning your trip is essential.
Advantages:

Convenience: Taxis and ridesharing services provide door-to-door service, particularly for airport transfers and city trips.

Safety: Using apps provides more excellent protection and fare transparency than street-hailing.

Tips

Licensed Taxis: Only use licensed taxis or reputed ridesharing services to safeguard your safety.

Cash: Keep modest amounts available for taxi payments, since not all drivers take credit cards.
Public Transportation
Urban buses and minibuses (combis) are widely used in cities. They are affordable but may need to be more straightforward for visitors.

Metropolitano: Lima's Bus Rapid Transit (BRT) system, Metropolitano, provides a quicker and more efficient means of getting around the city.

Advantages
Affordability: Public transportation is the most cost-effective way to move around cities.
Local Experience: Provides a genuine glimpse into everyday living in Peru.

Tips

Research Routes: To minimize misunderstanding, familiarize yourself with the bus routes and stops ahead.

Safety: Be mindful of your things, particularly in crowded cars.

Car Rentals

Availability: Rental cars are accessible in major cities and airports. Hertz, Avis, and Budget are international firms operating in Peru.

Requirements: A valid driver's license and credit card are necessary. International driving licenses are suggested but not required.

Advantages

Flexibility: Renting a vehicle allows you to explore rural locations independently.

Comfort: Ideal for families or parties who want more room and convenience.

Tips
Road Conditions: Be prepared for variable road conditions, particularly in rural and hilly regions.

Navigation: To navigate unknown roads, use GPS or a trusted map.

Understanding the transportation alternatives accessible in Peru allows you to choose the best ways for your itinerary, budget, and interests. Whether traveling between big cities, taking picturesque train trips, or visiting tiny neighborhoods by bus or taxi, getting to Peru is part of the experience that makes your trip unforgettable.

Chapter 2: Lima—The Vibrant Capital

2.1 Historical and Cultural Highlights of Lima.

Lima, Peru's capital city, is a thriving metropolis that combines ancient history, colonial architecture, and contemporary culture. Founded by the Spanish adventurer Francisco Pizarro in 1535, it swiftly rose to become the most important city in the Spanish Viceroyalty of Peru. Today, it serves as a symbol of the country's rich cultural legacy. Here are some of Lima's historical and cultural attractions that every tourist should see.

Historic Center of Lima

1. Plaza mayor (Plaza de Armas):
Plaza Mayor is the hub of colonial Lima, surrounded by some of the city's most notable structures.

Highlights:
Government Palace (Palacio de Gobierno): This stately structure on the plaza's north side serves as the President of Peru's official home. Visitors may see the ceremonial changing of the guard.

The Cathedral of Lima, located on the square's east side, started building in 1535. It displays a variety of architectural styles and houses Francisco Pizarro's mausoleum.

Lima's municipal hall, the Municipal Palace (Palacio Municipal), is situated on the west side of the square and has excellent colonial architecture.

2. The Monastery of San Francisco is also known as the Basilica and Convent of San Francisco.

Significance: This monastery is a prominent example of Spanish Baroque architecture, known for its beautiful woodwork and extensive catacombs.

Highlights:
Catacombs: One of colonial Lima's most incredible cemeteries, the catacombs hold the remains of around 70,000 individuals.
The monastery's library has an extensive collection of ancient literature and holy manuscripts.

3. Casa de Aliaga

Significance: One of Lima's earliest colonial homes, dated from 1535.

Highlights: The Aliaga family still occupies the home, and guided tours give insight into colonial life and design.

Cultural Institutions

1. The Larco Museum (Museo Larco)

Significance: The Larco Museum, located in an 18th-century viceroyal residence, is well-known for its rich collection of pre-Columbian artworks.

Highlights:

The Gold and Silver Gallery features a beautiful collection of antique jewelry and ceremonial relics.

The Erotic Gallery showcases an unusual collection of antique erotic ceramics.

The leading exhibitions include relics from pre-Columbian civilizations, including the Moche, Nazca, and Inca.

2. Museo de la Nación (National Museum)

Significance: One of Peru's major museums, it offers a thorough account of the country's history from antiquity to the present.

Highlights:

Permanent Exhibits: Focus on significant pre-Columbian civilizations and the effect of Spanish colonialism.

Temporary exhibits will focus on modern Peruvian art and culture.

3. MATE (Mario Testino Museum):

Significance: Dedicated to the work of renowned Peruvian fashion photographer Mario Testino.
Highlights include alternating exhibits of Testino's photography and works by other contemporary artists.

Cultural Districts
1. Barranco
Significance: Barranco, Lima's bohemian quarter, is known for its creative ambiance, vivid murals, and active nightlife.

Highlights:
Bridge of Sighs (Puente de los Suspiros): This lovely wooden bridge is a favorite destination for lovers and photographers.

Barranco's Main Square is surrounded by colonial-era buildings and lined with restaurants, bars, and galleries.
The Museo de Arte Contemporáneo (MAC) hosts exhibits of contemporary art from Peru and throughout the globe.

2. Miraflores
Significance: A lively region that mixes modernism and traditional charm while providing breathtaking coastline vistas.

Highlights:

Huaca Pucllana is a historic adobe and clay pyramid in Miraflores that dates back to the Lima period (200-700 AD).

Parque Kennedy: A central park surrounded by stores, cafés, and restaurants often holding art exhibits and cultural events.

Larcomar is a sophisticated retail mall constructed into the cliffs above the Pacific Ocean, providing eating, shopping, and entertainment with a view.

Religious and Architectural Landmarks

1. The Basilica and Convent of Santo Domingo
Significance: One of Lima's oldest and most significant religious sites, constructed in the 16th century.

Highlights:

Tomb of Saint Rose of Lima: The first saint of the Americas is buried with Saint Martin de Porres and Saint John Macias.
The Bell Tower offers sweeping views of Lima's historic center.

2. Church of San Pedro:
Significance: Built by the Jesuits in the 17th century, this church is an excellent example of Peruvian Baroque architecture.
Highlights include lavishly adorned interiors with gold leaf, ornate altarpieces, and religious artwork.

Culinary delights.
1. Peruvian Cuisine:
Significance: Lima is South America's gourmet capital, with a diversified culinary scene reflecting the country's rich cultural background.

Highlights:
Ceviche is Peru's national meal. It consists of fresh, raw fish marinated in citrus liquids and served with onions, maize, and sweet potato.
Lomo Saltado is a stir-fried meal with Peruvian and Chinese characteristics. It includes beef, tomatoes, onions, and fries.
Pisco Sour: The national drink, a cocktail created from pisco (a brandy), lime juice, syrup, egg white, and bitters.

2. Notable restaurants:
Central is ranked among the top restaurants in the world. It serves unique meals that reflect Peru's various ecosystems.
Maido is famous for its Nikkei cuisine, which combines Peruvian and Japanese tastes.

Astrid y Gastón: Located in a historic home, this restaurant is known for its modern spin on traditional Peruvian food.
By experiencing Lima's historical and cultural treasures, tourists may develop a profound understanding of the city's rich legacy and lively present. Lima provides a dynamic and exciting travel experience, whether you

meander through historical plazas, visit world-class museums, explore artsy districts, or sample local food.

2.2 Major Attractions: Miraflores, Barranco, and Centro Histórico

Lima, Peru's capital, is a city of contrasts, where old history meets modernity, and colonial architecture coexists with contemporary culture. The Miraflores, Barranco, and Centro Histórico districts each provide distinct attractions and experiences that represent the city's eclectic culture. Here's a detailed look at what each of these regions has to offer.

Miraflores

1. Huasca Pucllana
This pre-Inca adobe pyramid is from the Lima civilization (approximately 200-700 AD). It operated as both a ceremonial and administrative center.

Highlights:
Guided tours are available both during the day and at night and include information on the site's historical importance and current archeological work.
On-Site Museum: Displays objects discovered on the site, such as ceramics and textiles.

2. Parque Kennedy

Miraflores's primary park is named for the United States President. John F. Kennedy Square is a vibrant area surrounded by cafés, boutiques, and restaurants.

Highlights:
Artisan markets are frequented by local artists and craftspeople exhibiting their handcrafted wares.
Cat Park is well-known for its friendly stray cat population, which is cared for by the community.

3. Larcomar
A cliffside retail area with stunning views of the Pacific Ocean.

Highlights:
Shopping and Dining: A wide range of high-end boutiques, restaurants, and cafés.
Entertainment options include a movie theater, pubs, and clubs.
Ocean Views: An ideal location for a lovely stroll along the ocean, particularly around sunset.

4. El Malecon
A chain of parks along Miraflores' cliffs with spectacular ocean views.

Highlights:
The Parque del Amor (Park of Love) is famous for its mosaic walls and the renowned statue "El Beso" (The Kiss) by Victor Delfín.

Jogging and Biking routes: Popular outdoor sports with well-kept routes and workout spaces.

Paragliding: Adventurers may experience paragliding over the cliffs, providing beautiful coastline views.

5. Indian Market:
A bustling market with diverse traditional Peruvian goods and souvenirs.

Highlights:
Handicrafts include textiles, pottery, jewelry, and alpaca wool goods.

Bargaining: Visitors may hone their negotiating abilities while shopping for unique things.

Barranco
1. The Bridge of Sighs (Puente de los Suspiros)
This lovely wooden bridge is one of Barranco's most romantic locations.

Highlights:
Legend states that holding your breath while crossing the bridge may fulfill a desire.

Views: Provides stunning views of the surrounding region and the Pacific Ocean.

2. Barranco's Main Square (Plaza Municipal):

The core of Barranco is surrounded by colonial houses, cafés, and art galleries.

Highlights:
City Hall exemplifies magnificent colonial architecture. Local artists often show their works in the area, creating a vibrant cultural environment.

3. Museum of Contemporary Art (MAC)
A major contemporary art museum in Lima that exhibits works by Peruvian and foreign artists.

Highlights:
Rotating exhibitions highlight contemporary art in a variety of media.

Cultural Events: The museum often holds lectures, seminars, and film screenings.

4. Casa de la Literature Peruana
A cultural institution devoted to Peruvian literature set in a stunning historic structure.

Highlights:
Exhibits will focus on the works of renowned Peruvian authors.
Events include regular literary readings, talks, and workshops.

5. Bajada de Los Baños:
A picturesque path from Barranco's central plaza to the Pacific Ocean.

Highlights:
Street Art: The route is decorated with vibrant murals and street art.
Ocean Views: Offers a picturesque approach to the beach, ideal for a leisurely walk.

2.3 Gastronomy: Best Restaurants and Local Cuisines in Peru

Peruvian Cuisine is world-renowned for its variety and taste, reflecting the country's rich cultural background and wealth of fresh ingredients. Peruvian Cuisine provides a delicious variety of tastes and textures, ranging from traditional dishes based on indigenous Andean and Amazonian traditions to new innovations influenced by global culinary trends. Here is a comprehensive guide to Peru's greatest restaurants and must-try Cuisine.

Best Restaurants.
1. Central (lima):
Cuisine: Contemporary Peruvian
Central, led by chef Virgilio Martínez, is routinely recognized as one of the world's top restaurants. It serves a multi-course tasting menu highlighting Peru's unique ecosystems, with each dish including ingredients from various elevations and locations.

2. Maido (lima):
Cuisine: Nikkei (a Peruvian-Japanese mix)

Chef Mitsuharu Tsumura uses Japanese methods and Peruvian ingredients to produce unique and delectable meals. Maido's tasting menu combines sushi, ceviche, and other Nikkei dishes, earning it a place on Latin America's 50 Best Restaurants list.

3. Astrid and Gastón (lima):
Cuisine: Contemporary Peruvian
Astrid y Gastón was founded by famous chef Gastón Acurio, a pioneer of contemporary Peruvian Cuisine. The restaurant provides a quality dining experience with meals highlighting traditional Peruvian ingredients and culinary expertise.

4. Central Restaurante (lima):
Cuisine: Contemporary Peruvian
Chef Pedro Miguel Schiaffino honors Peru's biodiversity with a cuisine that includes indigenous Amazonian delicacies. Central Restaurant takes guests on a gourmet trip through the Amazon jungle, with dishes inspired by traditional Amazonian cooking techniques.

5. Malabar (lima):
Cuisine: Contemporary Peruvian
Chef Pedro Miguel Schiaffino uses Peruvian ingredients and worldwide inspirations to produce new and delectable meals. Malabar's Cuisine combines classic and contemporary Peruvian dishes, focusing on sustainability and seasonality.

6. La Mar (lima):
Cuisine: Peruvian seafood.

La Mar is known for its fresh fish meals and inventive ceviche varieties. The restaurant has a colorful and energetic ambiance and serves a diverse cuisine that highlights Peru's coastal culinary tradition.

7. Isolina (lima):
Cuisine: Criollo (traditional Peruvian).
Isolina offers substantial and tasty criollo food in a comfortable and relaxed atmosphere. The menu includes typical Peruvian meals like anticuchos (grilled skewers), causa (layered potato dish), and arroz con pato (duck with rice), all made using traditional methods and high-quality ingredients.

8. Maido (lima):
Cuisine: Nikkei (a Peruvian-Japanese mix)
Maido is known for its creative Nikkei cuisine, which combines Japanese methods with Peruvian ingredients. The restaurant's tasting menu features various tastes and textures, including sushi, sashimi, ceviche, and tiraditos.

9. Osso (lima):
Cuisine: steakhouse.
Osso is a popular location for meat enthusiasts. Its various high-quality cuts are perfectly grilled. The restaurant's hallmark dishes include dry-aged steaks, beef ribs, and gourmet burgers, all served with exquisite sides and sauces.

10. Panchita (lima):
Cuisine: Criollo (traditional Peruvian).

Panchita is a lively and busy restaurant specializing in criollo Cuisine, emphasizing traditional Peruvian recipes and spices. The menu includes staples like anticuchos, ceviche, lomo saltado, and regional delicacies from around Peru.

Must-try local dishes
1. **Ceviche**:
Ceviche, Peru's national Cuisine, marries fresh raw fish in lime juice, onions, chili peppers, and cilantro. It is usually served with sweet potatoes, maize, and roasted corn kernels (concha).

2. **Lomo saltado**
A traditional Peruvian stir-fry meal consists of marinated beef strips, onions, tomatoes, and peppers served with French fries and rice. It blends Chinese stir-fry methods with Peruvian ingredients.

3. **Anticuchos:**
Grilled skewers of marinated meat, often beef heart, served with boiled potatoes and hot chili sauce. Anticuchos are a popular street meal in Peru, particularly as a late-night snack.

4. **Aji De Gallina**:
A creamy chicken stew with shredded chicken, yellow chili peppers, bread, and walnuts simmered in a rich and spicy aji amarillo sauce.

5. Causa:

A layered potato dish prepared with mashed potatoes seasoned with lime juice and yellow chili pepper, filled with avocado, chicken salad, or seafood, and topped with hard-boiled eggs and olives.

6. Rocoto Relleno:

A spicy Peruvian meal created with rocoto peppers filled with a tasty mixture of ground beef, onions, garlic, raisins, and almonds, then covered with melted cheese and baked to perfection.

7. Pisco Sour:

Peru's national drink comprises pisco (grape brandy), lime juice, simple syrup, egg white, and Angostura bitters. It is shaken with ice and served in a cold glass garnished with a lime slice.

8. Cuy (guinea pig):

Cuy is a classic Andean dish that consists of roasted or fried guinea pigs served whole with potatoes and aji sauce. It is considered a delicacy in Peru and is widely consumed on special occasions and festivals.

9. Taco Tacu:

A delicious Peruvian meal created with leftover rice and beans combined and fried until crispy, it is served with a variety of toppings, including grilled meats, fried eggs, and salsa criolla.

2.4 Art and Entertainment: Museums, Theatres, and Nightlife

Lima, Peru's capital city, is noted for its historical importance and bustling arts and entertainment scene. It provides a diverse cultural experience for both tourists and inhabitants, with world-class museums, theaters exhibiting local and international talent, and nightlife to suit all tastes.

Museums

1. Museo Larco:
Museo Larco, located in Lima's Pueblo Libre sector, is one of the city's most recognized museums. It holds an extensive collection of pre-Columbian antiquities, including pottery, textiles, and gold and silver objects. The Erotic Gallery and the Gold and Silver Gallery are must-sees.

2. MALI (Art Museum of Lima):
MALI is Lima's principal art museum, with a rich collection of Peruvian art from pre-Columbian antiquity. The museum's exhibitions include paintings, sculptures, and decorative arts, offering a glimpse into Peru's rich cultural legacy.

3. Museum of the Nation:
Museo de la Nación, located in the San Borja area, explores Peruvian history and culture. The museum's exhibitions include archeology, anthropology, and modern art, giving visitors a broad insight into the country's unique background.

4. Museum of Contemporary Art (MAC)

MAC is a contemporary art museum that exhibits work by Peruvian and international artists. The museum's displays include a range of genres, including painting, sculpture, photography, and video, and provide insight into Peru's current art scene.

5. Museo Pedro de Osma:

Museo Pedro de Osma, located in the Barranco area, is a wonderfully preserved colonial palace. The museum's collection specializes in colonial and decorative arts, including displays of paintings, sculptures, furniture, and ceramics from the 16th to 19th centuries.

Theaters

1. **Theatre Municipal of Lima:** Teatro Municipal de Lima, founded in 1901, is one of the city's oldest and most prominent theaters. It presents opera, ballet, drama, and concerts by both local and foreign performers.

2. **Grand National Theatre:** The Gran Teatro Nacional is Peru's foremost performing arts theater. The cutting-edge theater showcases various shows, including opera, dance, drama, and symphonic concerts, including classic and modern works.

3. **Theatre La Plaza:** Teatro La Plaza, located in the Miraflores area, is a modern theater that features new and experimental performances by rising artists and theatre

organizations. The theatre's schedule includes a variety of plays, concerts, and workshops.

4. **Theatre Británico:** Teatro Británico, established in 2002, is a cultural facility committed to promoting the arts in Lima. The theater conducts various activities, including plays, concerts, film screenings, and workshops, all emphasizing cultural interaction between Britain and Peru.

5. **Teatro Segura:** Teatro Segura is a historic theater in Lima, notable for its neoclassical style and rich cultural legacy. The theater hosts a broad calendar of events, including plays, musicals, and concerts, which draw local and international audiences.

Nightlife

1. **Barranco:** Barranco is Lima's bohemian quarter, renowned for its active nightlife scene. The area has a profusion of pubs, clubs, and live music venues that play anything from jazz and salsa to techno and indie rock.

2. **Miraflores:** Miraflores is one of Lima's most prominent nightlife areas, offering a diverse selection of pubs, cafes, and nightclubs to suit all preferences. It also has a contemporary rooftop bar, a charming wine bar, and a high-energy dance club.

3. **Historical Center:** Lima's historic core comes alive at night with many clubs, cafés, and cultural institutions.

Visitors may relax with a drink in one of the landmark plazas, watch live music in a local pub, or discover the city's unique street art culture.

4. San Isidro: San Isidro is one of Lima's affluent areas, noted for its expensive clubs and lounges. Visitors may enjoy specialty drinks and excellent wines in upscale settings, with many locations including live music and DJ performances.

5. Surquillo:
Surquillo is a dynamic neighborhood noted for its thriving markets and exciting nightlife. Visitors may enjoy traditional Peruvian Cuisine at local restaurants, drink cocktails at fashionable bars, or dance at one of the district's many clubs and discos the night away.

2.5 Travel Tips for Accommodation and Safety

Assessing your lodging alternatives and emphasizing safety precautions is essential when visiting Peru to guarantee a smooth and pleasurable vacation. Here are some travel suggestions to help you plan your trip, including hotel options, safety considerations, and estimated accommodation rates.

Accommodation Options:
1. Hotels in Peru cater to various budgets and interests. From luxury resorts and boutique hotels to low-cost hostels and guesthouses, there is something for every

tourist. When picking a hotel, consider location, facilities, and customer reviews.

2. **Hostels:** Ideal for budget tourists and backpackers, hostels provide economical lodging in communal dormitory-style rooms or individual rooms. Many hostels have standard amenities such as kitchens, lounges, and planned activities, making them friendly and inexpensive.

3. **Airbnb:** Renting a private apartment or room on Airbnb may provide a more customized and immersive experience, particularly for extended visits. You may discover lodging in residential districts, enabling you to live like a local while exploring off-the-beaten-path locations.

4. **Guesthouses and Bed & Breakfasts:** These smaller, family-run facilities provide a comfortable and private setting, sometimes with individual service and home-cooked meals. Guesthouses and B&Bs are typical in rural regions and small towns, providing an opportunity to interact with people.

Safety precautions
1. **Secure Accommodation:** Choose lodging in secure and well-traveled locations, particularly if traveling alone or arriving late at night. Choose a respectable hotel, hostel, or guesthouse with safe locks, 24-hour reception, and security cameras.

2. **Use Safety Deposit Boxes:** To protect your belongings, use the safety deposit boxes or secure storage facilities

supplied by your hotel. Store essential papers, cash, and devices securely when not in use.

3. **Stay Informed:** Familiarize yourself with local safety regulations and emergency procedures. Keep up with current events, weather conditions, and possible risks in the regions you want to visit. Register with your embassy or consulate and have emergency contact information.

4. **Exercise Caution:** Be cautious while exploring unknown regions, particularly at night. Avoid exhibiting pricey items or flashing enormous sums of money. Use trustworthy transportation providers and be aware of fraud, pickpocketing, and tourist-targeted crimes.

Approximate Accommodation Prices
1. **Budget Accommodation (Hostels/Guesthouses):** Depending on location and facilities, dormitory beds or basic private rooms cost between $10 and USD 30 per night.

2. **Mid-Range housing (Hotels/Airbnb):** A standard double room in a mid-range hotel or private housing costs between $30 and USD 100 per night, with rates ranging depending on location and amenities.

3. **Luxury Accommodation (Resorts/High-End Hotels):** Luxury resorts, boutique hotels, or high-end properties may cost $100 to USD 500+ per night and provide premium facilities, breathtaking vistas, and unique services.

Prices are approximate and may fluctuate depending on seasons, location, and availability. Book your accommodations early to take advantage of the best pricing and selections, particularly during high travel seasons.

Consider these travel recommendations on housing options and safety measures to make educated selections that will improve your travel experience in Peru while assuring your comfort and security during your stay.

In southern Peru, the ancient city of Cusco exemplifies the Inca civilization's rich cultural history and the colonial effect of the Spanish invasion. Cusco, formerly the significant capital of the Inca Empire, is today a UNESCO World Heritage Site and a thriving center of culture, history, and beautiful architecture.

Chapter 3: Cusco and Sacred Valley

3.1 The Historical City of Cusco

Nestled in the Andes Mountains of southern Peru, the ancient city of Cusco exemplifies the Inca civilization's rich cultural history and the colonial effect of Spanish invasion. Cusco, formerly the significant capital of the Inca Empire, is a UNESCO World Heritage Site today and a thriving center of culture, history, and beautiful architecture. Here's a deeper look at the charm and importance of this lovely city.

Historical and Cultural Significance

1. Cusco was the Inca Empire's capital, known as "Qosqo" in Quechua, the Incas' native language. It functioned as the empire's political, religious, and administrative hub, with a grand plaza, temples, and palaces reflecting Inca culture's might and refinement.

2. **Spanish Conquest:** In 1533, Spanish conquistadors headed by Francisco Pizarro seized Cusco, establishing Spanish colonial power in Peru. The invaders demolished numerous Inca constructions and constructed churches, monasteries, and palaces on their foundations, resulting in a distinct combination of Inca and Spanish design.

3. Cusco's streets are dotted with architectural marvels, ranging from the vast stone walls of Sacsayhuamán to the delicately carved façade of colonial churches. Notable sites include the Plaza de Armas, the Cathedral of Santo Domingo, and the Temple of the Sun (Qorikancha), formerly Cusco's most famous Inca temple.

Cultural Heritage

1. **Indigenous Traditions:** Cusco has maintained numerous indigenous traditions and rituals despite centuries of colonialism. Many locals still speak Quechua, and ancient holidays and rituals like Inti Raymi (the Festival of the Sun) are widely celebrated.

2. Cusco is well-known for its bright artisan markets, where tourists can peruse colorful fabrics, complex ceramics, and handcrafted items. The San Pedro Market

is a thriving center of activity that sells everything from fresh fruit to traditional Andean trinkets.

3. **Museums and Galleries:** Cusco has many museums and galleries highlighting the city's rich cultural past. The Museo de Arte Precolombino has an outstanding collection of pre-Columbian antiquities, while the Centro Qosqo de Arte Nativo showcases traditional Andean music and dance.

3.2 Discovering the Sacred Valley: Pisac, Ollantaytambo, and Moray

The Sacred Valley of the Incas, situated in Peru's Andean highlands, is a breathtaking landscape rich in history, culture, and natural beauty. This rich valley, created by the Urubamba River, was once the heartland of the Inca Empire and now contains some of Peru's most stunning archeological monuments and thriving settlements. Pisac, Ollantaytambo, and Moray are key attractions in the Sacred Valley, each providing distinct experiences and insights into the Incas' rich past.

Pisac Markets and Terraces

1. Pisac Marketplace:
Pisac is well-known for its busy market in the main plaza. This bustling market is a must-see for visitors looking to immerse themselves in the local culture. Various handicrafts, textiles, jewelry, and fresh fruit are available here. The market is most busy on Sundays when

inhabitants from nearby settlements gather to sell their wares and engage in traditional festivities.

2. Pisac Ruins:
The Pisac ruins, which overlook the town, are a beautiful Inca complex that includes agricultural terraces, ceremonial baths, a sun temple, and a sophisticated system of stone structures and paths. The terraces, cut into the slope, are especially spectacular, demonstrating the Incas' superior farming practices and ability to adapt to the harsh Andean environment.

3. Hike and Views:
Hiking to the ruins offers stunning views of the Sacred Valley and surrounding mountains. The journey to the summit is challenging but rewarding, providing a closer look at the terraces and an appreciation for the magnitude and genius of Inca architecture.

Ollantaytambo: The Living Inca Town.

1. The Ollantaytambo Fortress:
Ollantaytambo is home to one of Peru's best-preserved Inca fortifications. The fortification doubled as a temple and a military stronghold, with vast stone terraces towering up the slope. The Temple of the Sun, the Enclosure of the Ten Niches, and the Princess' Baths are notable landmarks. The location also provides panoramic views of the town and valley below.

2. Living Inca Town:

Unlike many other Inca monuments, Ollantaytambo is a thriving town that has been inhabited since Inca times. Its cobblestone walkways, stone structures, and water systems remain intact, offering a rare view into medieval urban design and everyday life. Walking around the village, tourists may observe typical Andean residences and engage with inhabitants who still practice their ancient rituals.

3. Gateway to Machu Picchu:
Ollantaytambo is a vital beginning place for the trek to Machu Picchu. Many tourists ride the train from here to Aguas Calientes, the village at the foot of Machu Picchu. The train excursion provides stunning views of the Sacred Valley and the Urubamba River.

Moray: Agricultural Marvel
1. Moray terraces:
Moray is an archeological site notable for its distinctive circular terraces, which resemble gigantic amphitheaters. These concentric terraces sink into the soil, resulting in various microclimates. The Incas thought of Moray as an agricultural laboratory to experiment with different crops and growing conditions. The temperature differential between the top and lower terraces may be up to 15°C (27°F), demonstrating the creativity of Inca farming operations.

2. Ingenious Designs:
The terraces' design is both visually appealing and helpful. Each level represents a separate biological zone, enabling the Incas to grow crops in an identical site. This

novel use of space and climate manipulation illustrates the Incas' excellent grasp of agricultural and environmental control.

3. Scenic surroundings:
Moray is surrounded by undulating hills and snow-capped peaks, making it a beautiful place to visit. The quiet of the location, along with the architectural wonder of the terraces, provide visitors with a serene and meditative experience.

Exploring the Sacred Valley offers a deep dive into the core of Inca culture. From Pisac's colorful marketplaces and historic terraces to the living history and massive stronghold of Ollantaytambo and the innovative agricultural experiments at Moray, each site provides a distinct perspective on the Incas' triumphs and legacy. The Sacred Valley is a tribute to Peru's architectural and agricultural brilliance and a dynamic environment where past and present coexist, enabling visitors to interact with the country's rich cultural legacy.

3.3 Machu Picchu: Plan Your Visit

Machu Picchu, the famed Lost City of the Incas, is one of the most popular tourist sites in the world. Nestled high in Peru's Andes Mountains, this historic fortress provides a stunning view of the Inca civilization's complex architecture and culture. To get the most out of your visit to this UNESCO World Heritage Site, meticulous preparation is required. Here is a complete resource to help you plan your trip to Machu Picchu.

Getting To Machu Picchu

1. From Cuzco to Aguas Calientes:
Rail: The most popular and picturesque route to Machu Picchu is via rail. Peru Rail and Inca Rail provide numerous daily departures from Cusco (Poroy Station) or the Sacred Valley (Ollantaytambo Station) to Aguas Calientes, the town at the foot of Machu Picchu. The travel takes around 3-4 hours from Cusco and 1.5-2 hours from Ollantaytambo.

Trek: For the most daring, the Inca Trail, Salkantay Trek, and Lares Trek are multi-day walks through breathtaking Andean vistas culminating in Machu Picchu. These hikes need previous planning and physical preparedness.

2. From Aguas Calientes to Machu Picchu:
Bus: Shuttle buses often travel from Aguas Calientes to Machu Picchu's entrance. The journey takes around 25 minutes and is a handy and pleasant way to reach the destination.

Climb: You may also climb to Machu Picchu from Aguas Calientes. The trip lasts 1.5-2 hours and includes a difficult elevation, making it worthwhile for those who prefer to see the citadel on foot.

Ticket and Entry

1. Ticket types:
Machu Picchu only: Basic access to the significant archeological site.

Machu Picchu + Huayna Picchu: Admission to the leading site includes a hike to Huayna Picchu, the mountain that overlooks the citadel. This steep and challenging hike provides excellent vistas.

Machu Picchu + Mountain: This package includes admission to the main site and a hike to Machu Picchu Mountain, which provides panoramic views of the surrounding countryside.

2. Booking tickets:
Advance Purchase: Machu Picchu tickets are limited and must be bought in advance, particularly during high seasons (June to August). Tickets may be purchased

online via the official Machu Picchu website or at approved travel agents.

Time Slots: Entry tickets are assigned specific time slots to regulate visitors' flow. To prevent problems, be sure to arrive at the entrance on time.

What to bring

1. Essentials:
Passport: You must provide your passport and admittance ticket at the door.
Tickets: Please provide printed or digital copies of your admission and bus/train tickets.

Water & Snacks: Bring a reusable water bottle and some light snacks, as food and beverages are not offered on the archaeological site.

Comfortable attire: Wear comfortable, breathable hiking attire, and pack layers since the weather may change quickly.
Strong Walking Shoes: You'll need sturdy, comfortable shoes with a solid grip to navigate the rough terrain.
Sunscreen, a hat, and sunglasses can help you protect yourself from the fierce Andean sun.
Insect repellent is advised for protection against mosquitoes and other insects.

The best time to visit

1. Dry Season (May-September):
Pros: With clear skies and low rainfall, this is the best season to walk and explore Machu Picchu. The busiest months are June through August, when visitor numbers are at their peak.

Cons: Increased tourist numbers might result in congested circumstances at popular destinations.

2. Wet Season (October-April):
The pros are fewer visitors and lovely green scenery. The Inca Trail is closed for repair in February, although Machu Picchu remains accessible.
Cons: A higher likelihood of rain and gloomy weather may obscure vistas and make paths hazardous.

Explore Machu Picchu.

1. Guided tours:
Advantages: Hiring a guide may improve your visit by offering detailed information about the site's history, architecture, and importance. Guides may be booked in advance or hired at the entry.

Language Options: The guides are available in many languages, including English and Spanish.

2. Self-guided tours:
Flexibility: Exploring independently enables you to go at your speed and devote more time to exciting topics.

Preparation: Bring a thorough map or guidebook to assist you in navigating the site and comprehending the importance of the numerous buildings.

3. Key highlights:
Intihuatana Stone is a ceremonial stone with astrological and agricultural significance.

Temple of the Sun: A significant religious site with breathtaking scenery and beautiful craftsmanship.
Room of the Three Windows: A building with three trapezoidal windows that provide a panoramic view of the Sacred Plaza.
The Sacred Plaza is a central location surrounded by significant structures, such as the Main Temple and the Temple of the Three Windows.

Additional Tips

1. Acclimatization:
Altitude Sickness: Cusco is 3,400 meters (11,150 feet) high, whereas Machu Picchu is 2,430 meters (7,970 feet). To reduce the danger of altitude sickness, spend a few days acclimating in Cusco or the Sacred Valley before visiting Machu Picchu.

2. Respect the site.
Help protect Machu Picchu by following established trails without climbing on the ruins and not taking any artifacts or vegetation.

Follow all established signs and instructions while being considerate of other visitors and the delicate environment. Planning your trip to Machu Picchu with these suggestions will ensure a seamless, pleasurable, and fantastic experience at one of the world's most outstanding archeological sites.

3.4 Trekking Adventures: The Inca Trail and Alternative Routes

Peru's Sacred Valley provides some of the most thrilling trekking experiences in the world, with paths leading to the famed Machu Picchu. While the Inca Trail is the most well-known walk, numerous other paths provide equally magnificent scenery, fascinating cultural experiences, and a less congested way to the old Inca citadel. Here's a detailed look at the Inca Trail and its various ways.

The Inca Trail

The Inca Trail is a famous hiking path to Machu Picchu, known for its historical importance and breathtaking beauty. The route follows historic Inca pathways, passing through varied habitats, archeological sites, and spectacular mountain passes.
The most popular route is a four-day walk, although there is other two- and five-day options.

Highlights:
Sun Gate (Inti Punku): A highlight of the hike is Machu Picchu at dawn when you can enjoy a stunning vista of the citadel.

Wiñay Wayna, a well-preserved Inca monument at the trail's finish, has terraces and ritual baths.

Dead Woman's Pass (Warmiwañusqa) is the path's highest point at 4,215 meters (13,828 ft) and provides panoramic views of the surrounding mountains.

Preparation:

Permits: Few permits are available, and they sell out rapidly, frequently months in advance. You must arrange them through a licensed tour operator.

Physical Fitness: The hike is strenuous, with steep ascents and descents. Good physical fitness and acclimation to altitude are required.

Packing List: Bring strong hiking boots, layers of clothes for several weather conditions, rain gear, a sleeping bag, trekking poles, and personal things.

Alternative Routes

1. Salkantay Trek:

The Salkantay Trek is a popular alternative to the Inca Trail, renowned for its breathtaking natural landscape and rugged terrain. The route covers high mountain passes, thick cloud forests, and tiny Andean settlements.

Duration: Usually, five days and four nights.

Highlights:

Salkantay Pass is the trek's highest point, at 4,650 meters (15,255 feet), with stunning views of the snow-capped Salkantay Mountain.

Humantay Lake: A magnificent turquoise lake at the foot of Humantay Mountain.

Rainforest Descent: The track leads through tropical rainforests with varied vistas and ecosystems.

2. Lares Trek:

The Lares Trek provides a more cultural experience by passing through traditional Andean settlements. Trekkers can connect with people and observe their way of life. The path also includes stunning mountain vistas and thermal springs.

Duration: Typically, three to four days.

Highlights:
Lares Hot Springs: Natural hot springs where hikers may unwind after trekking.

Andean communities: Opportunities to explore and stay in local communities and learn about traditional weaving, farming, and everyday living.

Non-Touristy Experience: Less congested than the Inca Trail, allowing for a more serene and personal trekking experience.

3. Inca Jungle Trek:

The Inca Jungle Trek is a multisport experience that includes trekking, mountain biking, and optional sports like whitewater rafting and zip-lining. It provides a unique and daring approach to Machu Picchu.

Duration: Typically, four days.

Highlights:
Mountain biking involves riding downhill from the high Andes to the rainforest.

Cocalmayo Hot Springs: Natural hot springs where hikers may relax.

Variation of Activities: The combination of sports gives excitement and variation to the experience.

4. Choquequirao Trek:
Choquequirao, described as the "sister city" of Machu Picchu, is a distant and lesser-known Inca monument that provides a demanding and rewarding hike. The journey is challenging but offers breathtaking vistas and a feeling of adventure.

Duration: Typically, 8 to 9 days when paired with a journey to Machu Picchu.

Highlights:
Choquequirao Ruins: A large and spectacular Inca monument with fewer people, offering a more private experience.

Strenuous walk: The walk includes steep ascents and descents across different landscapes, making it suitable for experienced hikers.

Best time to trek:
The Dry Season (May to September) provides the most significant weather conditions, with clear skies and little rain. However, this is the busiest season.

Wet Season (October to April): Trails are less busy, and the scenery is lush and green, but there is a greater risk of rain, making trekking conditions more difficult.

Properly planning and preparing for your trekking expedition in the Sacred Valley allows you to enjoy Peru's unrivaled beauty and cultural diversity while creating lifelong memories. Whether you choose the renowned Inca Trail or one of the other ways, each road has its rewards and obstacles, providing a memorable trip to Machu Picchu.

3.5 Cultural Insights: Festivals, Markets, and Local Traditions

Peru has a rich cultural legacy, with a colorful tapestry of customs, festivals, and marketplaces that reflect its unique history and the impact of its indigenous and colonial pasts. Exploring these cultural components gives in-depth insights into Peruvians' everyday lives and spiritual beliefs. Here's a detailed look at some essential cultural things you should see while visiting Peru.

Festivals

1. Inti Raymi (The Festival of the Sun)
When: June 24.
Where: Cusco.
Inti Raymi is one of Peru's most important festivities. It marks the winter solstice and worships the Inca Sun God, Inti. The celebration features elaborate reenactments of Inca rites, colorful parades, music, and dancing. The major event takes place in Sacsayhuamán, an old castle where performers dressed in traditional costumes perform rites meant to guarantee bountiful harvests.

2. Carnaval:
When: February or March, before Lent.
Where: Nationwide, including noteworthy festivals in Puno and Cajamarca.
Peru's Carnaval is a vibrant and colorful holiday with parades, music, dancing, and ancient customs. In Puno, the event coincides with the Feast of the Virgin of Candelaria, resulting in a lively celebration of Catholic and indigenous customs. Cajamarca's celebrations are notable for their spectacular costumes, water bottles, and street parties.

3. The Lord of Miracles (Señor de los Milagros)
When: October.
Where: Lima.

Description: This religious celebration is one of the world's biggest processions, commemorating a 17th-century portrait of Christ that survived a catastrophic earthquake. Devotees dress in purple and carry the Lord of Miracles' picture through Lima's streets while singing hymns, praying, and burning incense. The celebration celebrates Peru's vital Catholic religion and historical links to Spain.

4. Qoyllur Rit'i (The Snow Star Festival):
When: Late May or early June.
Where: Sinakara Valley, near Cusco
This ancient Andean pilgrimage sees hundreds of people go to the Sinakara Valley to celebrate a miraculous picture of Christ that appears on a rock. The celebration combines indigenous and Christian components, including dances, music, and rituals conducted at high elevations, typically in snowy weather. It represents a powerful statement of religion and cultural identity for the Quechua people.

Markets
1. Pisac Marketplace:
When: Sundays (biggest); also runs on Tuesdays and Thursdays.
Where: Pisac, Sacred Valley.
The Pisac Market is one of Peru's most renowned. It offers a diverse selection of handicrafts, textiles, ceramics, jewelry, and fresh fruit. It's a terrific spot to acquire traditional Andean items like alpaca wool clothing, woven blankets, and silver jewelry. The market also offers an insight into local life, as farmers and artisans from nearby villages come to sell their wares.

2. San Pedro Market:
Where: Cusco.

When: Daily.

Description: San Pedro Market, located in Cusco's historic center, is a thriving bustle of activity. The market is organized into areas that offer fresh fruits and vegetables, meats and cheeses, and a variety of traditional dishes. It's a great spot to sample local cuisine, such as ceviche, empanadas, and fresh fruit drinks. The market also has booths offering souvenirs, apparel, and other items.

3. Market Central:
Where: Lima.
When: Daily.
Lima's central market is a bustling and chaotic site that reflects the city's cosmopolitanism. It's an excellent place to try a range of Peruvian cuisine, from street snacks to gourmet specialties. The market also sells spices, herbs, fish, and meats. For a truly local experience, go to the nearby streets, where informal sellers offer anything from gadgets to apparel.

4. Chinchero Market:
When: Sundays.
Where: Chinchero, Sacred Valley.
The Chinchero Market, famous for its high-quality textiles, is a must-see for anybody interested in traditional Andean weaving. Artisans showcase wonderfully woven fabrics, such as ponchos, shawls, and blankets, and often demonstrate conventional weaving processes. The market also sells farm items, providing a more personal and less touristic experience than some more significant markets.

Local traditions
1. Weaving & Textile:
Weaving is a deep-rooted Andean tradition, with skills and patterns handed down through generations. The vivid fabrics often include elaborate motifs representing parts of the natural world and Inca mythology. Visiting weaving cooperatives in locations like Chinchero or Ollantaytambo lets you see the careful process of producing these fabrics and acquiring original, handcrafted items.

2. Andean Music & Dance:
Music and dancing are essential aspects of Peruvian culture, and indigenous instruments such as the charango (a tiny Andean stringed instrument), quena (flute), and panpipes provide unique sounds. Folk dances, including the marinera, huayno, and diablada, often relate tales about love, work, and historical events. Festivals and cultural performances allow visitors to see these lively representations of Peruvian tradition.

3. Traditional Cuisine:
Peruvian cuisine combines indigenous ingredients and culinary traditions with Spanish, African, and Asian influences. Ceviche (fresh fish marinated in citrus juices), lomo saltado (stir-fried beef with vegetables), and pachamanca (meat and vegetables baked in an earthen oven) are some of the signature meals. Exploring local markets and eating at traditional eateries is a delightful way to discover Peru's culinary variety.

4. **Religious and spiritual practices:**

Peruvians often mix Catholicism with local spiritual traditions. Pachamama (Mother Earth) is honored, and rituals such as the payment to the earth ceremony (which involves donating coca leaves, food, and other objects to the soil) continue to be conducted, particularly in rural regions. Visiting holy locations and participating in these rites may bring remarkable insights into the spiritual lives of the Andeans.

Immersing oneself in Peru's festivals, marketplaces, and local customs provides an enriching and satisfying travel experience. The huge festivals of Inti Raymi, the lively kiosks of Pisac Market, and the delicate weavings of Andean artists all reflect the richness and complexity of Peruvian tradition. Exploring these features provides a better knowledge of the country's history, people, and ongoing customs.

Chapter 4: The Amazon Rainforest.

4.1 Introduction to the Peruvian Amazon.

The Peruvian Amazon, a vast and ecologically diverse area, is a substantial component of the larger Amazon Rainforest. This area covers more than 60% of Peru's territory and is well-known for its extraordinary biodiversity, indigenous cultures, and lonely, beautiful landscapes. Peru's Amazon Basin is separated into two areas: the lowland Amazon, with its thick jungle and river systems, and the highland Amazon, where the Andes meet the rainforest. This detailed introduction to the Peruvian Amazon focuses on its geography, biodiversity, cultural value, and significant locations.

Geography & Environment

1. Lowland Amazon:
The lowland Amazon is the Peruvian Amazon's largest and most diversified region. It is known for its lush, deep woods, many rivers, and broad floodplains. The climate is hot and humid, with heavy rains throughout the year.

Major Rivers: The Amazon River, created by the junction of the Ucayali and Maranon rivers, and other notable tributaries include the Napo, Madre de Dios, and Putumayo rivers.

2. Highland Amazon:
The highland Amazon, often known as the cloud forest, is formed when the Andes mountains fall into the Amazon Basin. This location has a distinct combination of a hilly landscape and deep, foggy trees.

Temperature: Because of the higher altitudes, the temperature is milder than in the lowland Amazon, although it is still humid and receives plenty of rain.

Biodiversity
1. Flora:
Rich Vegetation: The Peruvian Amazon is home to an incredible diversity of plant species, including towering ceiba trees, luscious palms, orchids, and various medicinal plants utilized by traditional populations.

Unique Ecosystems: Plants may thrive in various environments, including varzea (flooded woods), terra firme (non-flooded forests), and palm swamps.

2. Fauna:

Jaguars, tapirs, giant otters, and many monkey species, including howler monkeys and capuchins, are among the region's famous animals.

Birds: Over 1,800 species live in the Peruvian Amazon, including beautiful macaws, toucans, and the elusive harpy eagle.

Reptiles and Amphibians: The Amazon is home to various reptiles, including anacondas and caimans, and amphibians like poison dart frogs and tree frogs.

Insects: The insect variety is astounding, with many kinds of butterflies, beetles, ants, and other invertebrates performing critical environmental roles.

Indigenous cultures
1. Ethnic Diversity:

Indigenous communities: The Peruvian Amazon is home to several indigenous communities, each with its language, rituals, and traditions. The Asháninka, Shipibo-Conibo, Yagua, and Aguaruna are some of the most prominent tribes.

Cultural Practices: These communities preserve a rich cultural heritage, which includes traditional crafts, music, dance, and spiritual rites that are profoundly rooted in their natural settings.

2. Sustainable living:
Traditional Knowledge: Indigenous people have significant knowledge of the rainforest's flora and animals, including medicinal plants and sustainable hunting and fishing methods.

Conservation initiatives: Many indigenous tribes actively participate in conservation initiatives, working to safeguard their land and way of life from dangers such as deforestation and illicit mining.

Key Destinations
1. Iquitos:
Iquitos is the biggest city in the Peruvian Amazon and can only be reached by boat or airplane. It is a significant entryway to explore the northern Amazon.

Sights: Popular sights include the Belén Floating Market, the Amazon Rescue Center for Manatees, and the Pacaya-Samiria National Reserve, which is noted for its incredible biodiversity.

2. Puerto Maldonado:
Puerto Maldonado, located in the southern Amazon, is another crucial entrance point for Amazon research. The city is accessible by both road and air.

Nearby attractions include the Tambopata National Reserve and the Manu National Park, which provide excellent possibilities for animal observation, bird watching, and immersion in natural rainforest habitats.

3. Manu National Park:

Manu National Park is a UNESCO World Heritage Site and one of the most biodiverse areas on the planet. It covers a large territory, from the Andean altitudes to the Amazon lowlands.

Activities: Visitors may visit a variety of environments, from cloud forests to lowland rainforests, and see a wide range of species.

4. Tambopata National Reserve.

Tambopata National Reserve near Puerto Maldonado is well-known for its extraordinary biodiversity. It serves as a sanctuary for both ecotourists and scholars.

Highlights: The reserve is famed for its clay licks, where hundreds of macaws and parrots congregate to feast on the mineral-rich clay. It also provides fantastic opportunities for guided forest walks, boat excursions, and canopy tours.

Ecotourism and conservation

1. Ecotourism:

Sustainable Travel: The Peruvian Amazon is a popular ecotourism destination, encouraging sustainable tourism that benefits local people and conservation initiatives.

Lodges and Tours: Many eco-lodges and tour companies provide guided excursions that offer immersive experiences in the rainforest while adhering to ecologically acceptable methods.

2. Conservation efforts:

Protected Areas: Peru has created several protected areas and national parks to conserve the Amazon's diverse wildlife. These measures are critical for addressing deforestation, illicit logging, and wildlife trafficking.

Community Involvement: Indigenous and local communities play an essential role in conservation, collaborating with NGOs and government agencies to safeguard ancestral lands and foster sustainable lifestyles.

The Peruvian Amazon is a treasure trove of natural beauty, cultural riches, and unrivaled biodiversity. From towering trees and varied animals to lively Indigenous cultures and substantial conservation initiatives, this area provides guests with a one-of-a-kind and profound experience. Whether experiencing the busy city of Iquitos, hiking through the pristine Manu National Park, or learning from indigenous tribes, the Peruvian Amazon offers many chances for adventure, exploration, and a better knowledge of one of the world's most important ecosystems.

4.2 Iquitos and Surroundings

Iquitos, the biggest city in the Peruvian Amazon and one of the world's largest towns inaccessible by road serves as a busy entryway to the Amazon jungle. Located on the banks of the Amazon, Nanay, and Itaya rivers, Iquitos is a thriving city rich in history, culture, and natural beauty. Visitors to the town and its surrounding environs may enjoy various activities, from exploring the complex rivers of the Amazon Basin to immersing themselves in the region's distinct cultural legacy.

Iquitos: The Heart of the Amazon.

1. History & Culture:
The rubber boom transformed Iquitos dramatically throughout the late nineteenth and early twentieth centuries. This time, it brought enormous riches to the city, as seen by its architecture, including Gustave Eiffel's Iron House (Casa de Fierro).

Cultural Melting Pot: During the rubber boom period, Iquitos had an inflow of people from all over the globe, resulting in a unique cultural combination. This variety is reflected in its food, music, and festivals.

2. Key attractions:

Belén Floating Market: A lively market with diverse local goods, traditional remedies, and unusual cuisine. The market is in the Belén area, where many buildings are constructed on stilts or rafts to withstand periodic floods.

Amazon Rescue Facility

This facility is dedicated to rescuing, rehabilitating, and releasing endangered Amazonian species, notably manatees. Visitors may learn about conservation initiatives and interact with rescued animals.

The Museum of Indigenous Amazonian Cultures displays artifacts and exhibits from several indigenous communities in the Amazon, providing insight into their traditions, crafts, and ways of life.

1. Pacaya–Samiria National Reserve:

One of Peru's most significant protected areas, comprising more than 20,000 square kilometers (7,700 square miles). It is also known as the "Jungle of Mirrors" because of the mirrored canals during the high-water season.

Biodiversity: Pink river dolphins, gigantic river otters, jaguars, and various bird species call this place home. The reserve also supports multiple plant species, including enormous ceiba trees and exquisite orchids.

Visitors may take guided boat cruises, animal viewing expeditions, and jungle trekking. Night excursions allow you to witness nocturnal species and see the environment in a new light.

2. Quistococha Tourism Complex:

This complex, approximately 6 kilometers (4 miles) from Iquitos, has an artificial lagoon, a small zoo, and a botanical garden.

Activities include swimming, paddle boating, and touring the zoo, home to monkeys, jaguars, and anacondas. The botanical garden shows a wide range of Amazonian plant species.

3. Pilintuwasi Butterfly Farm and Animal Orphanage:

Description: This institution, located in the community of Padre Cocha, functions as both a butterfly farm and an animal orphanage, emphasizing conservation and education.

Activities: Guided tours teach about the life cycle of butterflies and the attempts to rehabilitate rescued creatures such as monkeys, ocelots, and anteaters.

4. Yaguas National Park:

A freshly constructed national park with 8,600 square kilometers (3,300 square miles) of natural rainforest.

Biodiversity: The park supports a diverse range of animals, birds, reptiles, and amphibians, many of which are endemic or vulnerable. It also promotes crucial biological processes and habitats.

Guided tours and eco-lodges provide chances to enjoy the park's abundant biodiversity, such as bird viewing, animal tracking, and river excursions.

Indigenous Community and Cultural Experiences
1. Visit Indigenous Communities:
Several trips visit indigenous villages in the Iquitos region. These excursions provide insight into Amazonian indigenous peoples' traditional lives, rituals, and crafts. Activities include cultural exchanges, traditional hunting and fishing practices, and artisan displays such as ceramics and weaving. It is essential to choose ethical tours that value and assist local communities.

2. Shamanic practices and ayahuasca ceremonies:
The Amazon is famed for its rich shamanic traditions, and Iquitos has become a spiritual tourist hotspot, especially for people seeking ayahuasca rituals. Ayahuasca, a traditional medicinal drink derived from native plants, is used in shamanic rituals to promote healing and spiritual awakening.

Activities: Many lodges and retreat facilities offer organized ayahuasca sessions led by skilled shamans. It is critical to approach these rituals respectfully and choose credible and ethical practitioners.

Practical information.
1. Getting there:
Air Travel: Regular flights from Lima and other major Peruvian towns connect Iquitos to the rest of Peru. The Coronel FAP Francisco Secada Vignetta International Airport (IQT) is the primary gateway.

River Travel: While only practicable for some visitors, Iquitos may be reached by riverboat from various sites, including the Brazilian border and other spots along the Amazon River.

2. Accommodation:

Iquitos offers various lodgings, from inexpensive hostels to luxury hotels. Many eco-lodges and jungle resorts are built along rivers, providing immersive rainforest experiences.

Eco-lodges: Numerous eco-lodges in the surrounding jungle welcome ecotourists with packages that include guided tours, animal excursions, and cultural experiences. Prices vary according to the degree of comfort and various activities available.

3. Health & Safety:

Immunizations: Travelers should ensure they are current on all immunizations, mainly yellow fever, which is advised in the Amazon area. Consult a travel health professional for information on required vaccines and prescriptions.

Mosquito Protection: The Amazon is a hotspot for mosquito-borne illnesses, including malaria and dengue fever. Apply insect repellent, wear long-sleeved clothes, and sleep beneath mosquito netting.

Water and Food: To prevent gastrointestinal difficulties, drink bottled or filtered water and use caution while eating. Eat well-cooked meals and avoid raw or undercooked foods.

Conclusion

Iquitos and its neighboring environs provide a remarkable combination of natural beauty, wildlife, and cultural richness. The Peruvian Amazon offers a one-of-a-kind and fantastic trip, whether you explore the enormous Pacaya-Samiria National Reserve, interact with indigenous villages, or immerse yourself in Iquitos' bustling city life. This region's deep connection to nature and traditional ways of living offers a unique chance to see one of the world's most spectacular ecosystems firsthand.

4.3 Puerto Maldonado and Tambopata Reserve

Puerto Maldonado, the capital of the Madre de Dios province in southeastern Peru, is a thriving gateway to the Amazon jungle. It is known for its abundant biodiversity and proximity to various protected areas. Puerto Maldonado is also the primary gateway to the world-famous Tambopata National Reserve. This location is an ecotourist's dream, with multiple activities and experiences emphasizing the Amazon's natural beauty and ecological value.

Puerto Maldonado: Gateway to Amazon

Puerto Maldonado is located at the junction of the Tambopata and Madre de Dios rivers, with easy access to the surrounding jungle and waterways.

Climate: The city has a tropical rainforest climate, with high humidity and heavy rains all year. Temperatures typically range from 25°C to 30°C (77°F to 86°F).

History & Culture
Rubber Boom: Like Iquitos, Puerto Maldonado saw expansion during the rubber boom period, but on a lesser scale. The town has now grown into a thriving hub for ecotourism.

Cultural Diversity: The area is home to indigenous groups, mestizo people, and new immigrants. This cultural variety is evident in local festivals, food, and everyday life.

Key attractions in Puerto Maldonado:

Plaza de Armas: Puerto Maldonado's major plaza is an excellent starting point for touring the city. It has a clock tower and several monuments honoring local history and culture.

Puente Billinghurst: This bridge across the Madre de Dios River provides panoramic views of the river and adjacent jungle. It is among the longest bridges in the Peruvian Amazon.

Markets & Local Cuisine: The markets are active and offer various Amazonian products, such as unusual fruits, seafood, and traditional cuisine. Visitors must try the local food.

Tambopata National Reserve
Tambopata National Reserve was formed in 1990 and has roughly 274,690 hectares (1,060 square miles) of protected rainforest.

Ecological significance: The reserve is part of the broader Madre de Dios area, noted for its unique biodiversity and distinct habitats. It is critical to the conservation of many species of flora and wildlife.

Biodiversity:
Animals: The Tambopata Reserve is home to an incredible diversity of animals, including jaguars, gigantic river otters, capybaras, monkeys (such as howler monkeys and spider monkeys), and over 600 bird species, including macaws, toucans, and harpy eagles.

Plants: The reserve's flora includes enormous ceiba trees, Brazil nut trees, orchids, and other medicinal plants utilized by indigenous peoples.

Habitats: The reserve has a variety of habitats, ranging from terra firme forests (non-flooded woods) to seasonally flooded varzea forests, each supporting a unique set of species and biological processes.

Activities & Experiences:
Animals Watching: Guided excursions allow one to see the reserve's rich animals. Bird viewing is viral, with many species visible in their native settings.

Clay Licks (Collpas): The reserve is well-known for its clay licks, where hundreds of macaws and parrots come to eat mineral-rich clay. The Chuncho and Colorado clay licks are among the most popular destinations.

Jungle treks: Visitors may take guided tours in the jungle, learning about the complex ecosystems and interrelationships between species.

Canopy Tours: Walkways and observation platforms erected high in the forest canopy provide a unique view of the rainforest and its inhabitants. These trips are ideal for seeing birds and other arboreal species.

River Excursions: Boat rides along the Tambopata and Madre de Dios rivers provide opportunities to observe aquatic species and gorgeous riverbank flora. Sunset and nighttime expeditions are very beneficial for viewing nocturnal species.

Eco-lodges:

Accommodation Options: Several eco-lodges in and around the reserve provide comfortable lodgings and authentic rainforest experiences. These lodges vary from basic to luxurious, catering to various tastes and budgets.

Sustainable methods: Many eco-lodges prioritize sustainability by implementing eco-friendly methods such as solar electricity, rainwater harvesting, and garbage management. They often collaborate with local communities to promote conservation and responsible tourism.

Conservation and Community Involvement
1. Conservation efforts:

Protected Areas: Creating the Tambopata National Reserve and other protected areas in the Madre de Dios region is essential in preserving Amazon biodiversity.

Ongoing research and monitoring initiatives help track animal populations, analyze ecological processes, and evaluate the environmental effects of human activities.

2. Community involvement:

Indigenous people: Conservation efforts rely heavily on indigenous people living in and around the reserve. Their traditional knowledge and ecological methods help to preserve the rainforest.

Many ecotourism programs engage local communities, providing them with sustainable incomes while encouraging the conservation of natural resources. These programs often feature community-run hotels, guided tours, and artisan fairs.

Practical information.

1. Getting there:

By Air: Puerto Maldonado has daily flights from Lima and Cusco. Padre Aldamiz International Airport (PEM) serves as the primary gateway.

By Road: For those looking for an overland adventure, the Interoceanic Highway links Puerto Maldonado and Cusco, offering an alternate route through the Andes and jungle.

2. Health & Safety:

Immunizations: Travelers should ensure they are current on all immunizations, mainly yellow fever, which is advised in the Amazon area. Consult a travel health professional for information on required vaccines and prescriptions.

Mosquito Protection: The Amazon is a hotspot for mosquito-borne illnesses, including malaria and dengue fever. Apply insect repellent, wear long-sleeved clothes, and sleep beneath mosquito netting.

Water and Food: To prevent gastrointestinal difficulties, drink bottled or filtered water and use caution while eating. Eat well-cooked meals and avoid raw or undercooked foods.

Puerto Maldonado and the Tambopata National Reserve provide a unique and immersive experience in the middle of the Amazon rainforest. From Puerto Maldonado's vibrant marketplaces and cultural attractions to Tambopata's rich biodiversity and pristine landscapes, this area offers limitless adventure, exploration, and conservation options.

4.4 Wildlife and Ecotourism

Peru's numerous habitats, spanning from the Amazon rainforest to the Andes Mountains, make it a popular destination for animal lovers and ecotourists. The country is home to an incredible diversity of flora and wildlife, including several indigenous and endangered species. Ecotourism in Peru offers unique and immersive natural experiences, encourages conservation efforts, and helps local people. This comprehensive reference to wildlife and ecotourism in Peru emphasizes significant locations, species, and environmentally beneficial methods.

Critical Regions for Wildlife and Ecotourism

1. The Amazon Rainforest
The Peruvian Amazon is divided into three regions: Madre de Dios, Loreto, and Ucayali. Tambopata National Reserve, Pacaya-Samiria National Reserve, and Manu National Park are essential conservation sites.

Wildlife: The Amazon is known for its biodiversity, including jaguars, substantial river otters, pink river dolphins, capybaras, a variety of monkey species, and over 1,800 bird species, including macaws and harpy eagles.

Popular ecotourism activities include guided forest treks, animal observation, boat trips, canopy walks, and visits to indigenous villages. Eco-lodges provide immersive experiences while minimizing environmental effects.

2. Andes Mountains:

Regions: The Andes include Cusco, Arequipa, and Ancash. The Sacred Valley, Colca Canyon, and Huascarán National Park are notable destinations.

Wildlife in the Andes includes the Andean condor, vicuña, spectacled bear, and various high-altitude bird species.

Ecotourism activities include hiking (including the Inca Trail), bird watching, mountain climbing, and cultural trips that emphasize the region's ancient sites and indigenous customs.

3. Coastal and marine areas:

Key coastal locations include the Paracas National Reserve, the Ballestas Islands, and the northern beaches of Tumbes and Piura.

Coastal and marine animals include Humboldt penguins, sea lions, dolphins, humpback whales, and various seabirds.

Ecotourism activities include boat trips, whale viewing, snorkeling, scuba diving, and visiting protected marine reserves.

Iconic species and where to find them.

1. Jaguars:

Tambopata National Reserve and Manu National Park are both located in the Amazon.

The best time to see wildlife is during the dry season (May to October) when it is more concentrated near water sources.

2. Andean condors:

Locations include Colca Canyon in Arequipa and the Sacred Valley in Cusco.

The best time to see condors is early dawn, when they are most active, flying on thermal currents.

3. Gigantic River Otters:

Locations include Lake Sandoval in Tambopata National Reserve and oxbow lakes in Manu National Park.

Best Time to See: Throughout the year, especially during the dry season.

4. Pink River Dolphins:

Locations include The Amazon River and its tributaries in Loreto and Madre de Dios.

The best time to see dolphins is during the dry season, when water levels are lower and they are more visible.

5. Humboldt Penguins:

Locations include Ballestas Islands and Paracas National Reserve.

Best Time to See: All year, with a larger concentration during the nesting season (April-October).

6. Spectacled Bears:

Locations include Andean cloud forests, notably those around Machu Picchu and northern Peru.

The best time to see them is during the dry season, when they are more active and more straightforward to trace.

Environmentally Friendly Practices in Wildlife Tourism

1. Sustainable lodging:

Many eco-lodges in Peru promote sustainability by implementing solar power, rainwater harvesting, garbage recycling, and the use of biodegradable materials.

Community Involvement: Eco-lodges often partner with local communities to provide jobs and promote conservation efforts.

2. Responsible Wildlife Viewing:

Guided Tours: Using qualified local guides minimizes animal disturbance and improves visitor awareness of the environment.

Code of Conduct: Following standards such as keeping a safe distance from animals, not feeding wildlife, and avoiding loud sounds may help safeguard animal habitats and habits.

3. Conservation Programs:

Research and Monitoring: Many ecotourism companies sponsor scientific research and animal monitoring programs, which provide essential data for conservation efforts.

Protected places: Visiting national parks and reserves helps to support conservation efforts and preserves protected places.

4. Supporting Local Communities:

Cultural tourism involves engaging with indigenous and local people via cultural tours, artisan markets, and homestays, encouraging sustainable development and preserving traditional knowledge.

Fair Trade: Buying locally created items and supporting community-run tourist programs helps the local economy.

Notable Ecotourism Destinations and Activities
1. Tambopata National Reserve.
Activities include jungle hikes, bird viewing, clay lick tours, night safaris, and river excursions.
Lodges: Many eco-lodges provide authentic rainforest experiences with knowledgeable guides.

2. Manu National Park:
Activities include multi-day trips, animal photography, bird viewing, and cultural visits to indigenous tribes.
Lodges: Remote lodges and research stations allow access to the park's most pristine parts.

3. Huascarán National Park:
Activities include trekking the Santa Cruz and Llanganuco circuits, mountain climbing, and high-altitude bird observation.
Features include stunning glacier vistas, high-altitude lakes, and diverse flora and fauna.

4. Paracas National Reserve and the Ballestas Islands:
Activities include boat cruises, bird watching, observing marine animals, and visiting the barren terrain of the Paracas Peninsula.
Wildlife includes sea lions, Humboldt penguins, dolphins, and various seabirds.

5. Sacred Valley and Machu Picchu:

Activities include hiking (including the Inca Trail), cultural excursions, and bird viewing.
Wildlife includes spectacled bears, Andean condors, and a variety of bird species in the cloud forests.

Practical Tips for Ecotourism
1. Plan:
Permits: Some sites, such as the Inca Trail and some sections of national parks, need permits. Book well in advance, particularly during high seasons.
Health Precautions: Make sure you have the proper vaccines and prescriptions. Pack bug repellant, sunscreen, and water purification pills.

2. **Pack responsibly:**
Environmentally Friendly Products: Use biodegradable toiletries and reusable water bottles and bags.
Appropriate Gear: Bring climate-appropriate clothes, sturdy footwear, and animal-watching binoculars.

3. **Respect local cultures.**
Learn Basic Phrases: Knowing a few phrases in Spanish or the local language will help you engage with people in your community.
Cultural Sensitivity: Respect local norms, dress modestly in traditional settings and always get permission before photographing individuals.
Conclusion

Peru's outstanding natural vistas and abundant biodiversity make it a top destination for wildlife and ecotourism. Peru's lush rainforests, high Andean peaks, and various marine habitats provide an unequaled opportunity to see nature in its purest form. Visitors who choose sustainable travel alternatives and support local conservation initiatives may help preserve these fantastic habitats for future generations while having beautiful experiences.

4.5 Rainforest Travel Tips: Health and Safety

Exploring the Amazon jungle is an exhilarating trip that provides unforgettable interactions with nature. However, the rainforest is a challenging environment, and being well-prepared is essential for a safe and pleasurable journey. Here are some important health and safety guidelines when visiting the jungle.

Health precautions
1. Vaccination and Medication:
Tourists entering the Amazon are strongly advised to get a yellow fever vaccine at least ten days before their travel. **Malaria Prophylaxis:** Because malaria is prevalent in certain sections of the Amazon, talk to your doctor about taking anti-malarial medicine. Follow the specified regimen as instructed.

Other immunizations: Ensure you have up-to-date standard immunizations, such as hepatitis A and B, typhoid, tetanus, and rabies, particularly if you intend to spend extended time in isolated places.

2. Mosquito Protection:
Insect Repellent: Apply a high-quality insect repellent that contains DEET, picaridin, or lemon eucalyptus oil. Reapply often, particularly after swimming or sweating.
To avoid exposing skin, wear long-sleeved shirts, long trousers, socks, and closed shoes. Tuck pants into socks and shirts into pants.

Mosquito Nets: Sleep beneath mosquito nets, particularly in open or unscreened rooms. Ensure that the nets surrounding your sleeping space are intact and firmly fastened.

3. Water and Food Safety:
Drink Purified Water: Always consume bottled, boiled, or chemically treated water. Avoid ice cubes, which may be created from untreated water.

Eating Safely: Consume prepared foods and avoid raw or undercooked meat, fish, or eggs. Be wary of salads and fruits that may have been washed in polluted water.
Personal Hygiene: Wash your hands often with soap and water, or use hand sanitizer when soap and water are unavailable.

Safety Tips
1. Guided Tours and Trusted Operators

Local Guides: Always employ expert guides familiar with the landscape, fauna, and any risks. They may provide crucial information and improve your safety.
Choose reliable tour providers that have received positive feedback and have a proven track record of safety. They should offer appropriate safety equipment and adhere to best practices for sustainable tourism.

2. Navigation & Communication:
Stay with Your Group: Getting lost in the lush jungle is easy, so always walk off with others. Stay with your group and follow your guide's directions.

Communication Devices: Carry a fully charged phone with emergency contact information. Consider carrying a satellite phone or a personal locating beacon (PLB) in isolated places.

3. Wildlife Safety:
Observe from a Safe Distance: Respect animals and keep your distance. Avoid approaching or touching animals since they are unpredictable and sometimes harmful.

Follow the rules: Stick to the rules supplied by your guide, particularly in regions notorious for poisonous snakes, insects, and other potentially dangerous creatures.

4. Weather and Environmental Hazards:
Rain Protection: The rainforest is a wet habitat, as the name implies. Bring waterproof clothing, such as a rain

jacket and a dry bag for valuables. Quick-drying clothing is also advised.

Heat and humidity: Stay hydrated and take breaks to prevent heat exhaustion. Wear a wide-brimmed hat and apply sunscreen to protect yourself from the sun.

Flooding and Rivers: Be careful near rivers, especially after heavy rain, since flash floods may occur. Follow your guide's recommendations for safe swimming areas and avoid fast-moving water.

5. First Aid Kits:
Basic Supplies: Keep a well-stocked first-aid kit with bandages, antiseptic wipes, tweezers, pain medicines, antihistamines, and any personal meds.

Emergency pills: Include pills for common ailments, including diarrhea, allergies, and motion sickness. Consult your doctor for suitable treatments for Amazon-specific dangers.

Packing Essentials
1. Clothing and gear:
Wear lightweight, breathable materials that wick sweat and dry quickly to feel comfortable in a humid atmosphere.

Wear robust, waterproof hiking boots or shoes with a solid grip. Also, bring appropriate sandals or water shoes for river activities.

Sun Protection: To protect yourself from the harsh tropical sun, pack a hat, sunglasses, and high-SPF sunscreen.

2. Equipment & Accessories:

Bring binoculars to view wildlife and a protective case camera to capture the incredible biodiversity.

Backpack: Use a comfy, water-resistant backpack to carry your necessities on outings.

Reusable Water Bottle: Stay hydrated with a reusable water bottle, particularly one with a built-in filter.

3. Personal Comfort Items:

Reusable Wet Wipes: Handy for fast clean-ups and preserving hygiene.

Travel Towel: A quick-drying travel towel is ideal for drying up after rain or river activities.

Books or Journals: Bring reading materials or a journal to capture your rainforest experiences.

Conclusion

Visiting the Amazon rainforest is an unforgettable experience that necessitates meticulous planning to ensure your health and safety. By taking the necessary precautions, listening to expert advice, and respecting the natural environment, you can have an unforgettable adventure in one of the world's most biodiverse regions. Proper planning and mindful practices will help you make the most of your journey while minimizing risks and supporting the conservation of this unique ecosystem.

Chapter 5: The South Coast and Desert

5.1 *The Nazca Lines: Mystery and Exploration.*

The Nazca Lines, a series of gigantic geoglyphs carved into the desert plains of southern Peru, are one of the world's most mysterious and awe-inspiring archeological marvels. These ancient patterns, located roughly 400 kilometers south of Lima, encompass around 450 square kilometers of the parched Nazca desert. For decades, academics and tourists have been captivated by the lines' purpose and construction, which take the form of numerous objects such as animals, vegetation, and geometric patterns.

Discovery and Research
1. **Early observations:**
The Nazca Lines originally received extensive notice in the early twentieth century. Toribio Mejía Xesspe, a Peruvian archaeologist, discovered them in 1927. However, it wasn't until commercial air travel that their entire extent and intricacy became apparent.

Aerial View: From the ground, the lines are almost identical. However, from above, the sheer scale and complexity of the decorations become clear. This airborne viewpoint has been critical for researching and charting the geoglyphs.

2. Key researchers:
Paul Kosok, an American historian and archaeologist, was among the first to research the Nazca Lines comprehensively. In the late 1930s, he proposed that the lines served astronomical and calendar functions.

Maria Reiche, a German mathematician and archaeologist, devoted her life to researching and conserving the Nazca Lines. She suggested that the geoglyphs represented a substantial astronomical calendar utilized by the ancient Nazca society.

The geoglyphs
1. Types of Design:
Animal Figures: The most well-known designs are the hummingbird, spider, monkey, fish, llama, lizard, and condor. These numbers are 50 to 300 meters long.

Geometric forms: The geoglyphs include a variety of lines and forms, including spirals, trapezoids, triangles, and straight lines that run for many kilometers.

Anthropomorphic forms: Less frequent but equally interesting are human-like forms, such as "The Astronaut," which has a humanoid shape and what looks to be a big head or helmet.

2. Creation Techniques:
The Nazca Lines were formed by removing the top layer of reddish-brown iron oxide-coated stones, exposing the lighter-colored dirt underneath. This strategy, paired with the region's dry and windless environment, has managed to maintain the lines for more than a millennium.

The specific equipment and workforce utilized are unclear, although basic surveying procedures and implements made of wood and stone were thought to be used. The accuracy and size of the lines indicate a well-organized and competent crew.

Theories & Interpretations
1. Astronomical calendar:
Alignment: Some academics think the lines correspond to astronomical events like solstices and equinoxes. Specific figures and lines may have indicated significant celestial occurrences, facilitating agricultural and ceremonial activity.

Reiche's Hypothesis: Maria Reiche staunchly supported this idea, claiming that the geoglyphs operated as an astronomical calendar, allowing the Nazca people to foresee seasonal changes.

2. Religious and ceremonial purposes:
Ritual routes: Another interpretation holds that the lines served as ritual routes. The Nazca people may have walked along the lines during religious rites, presumably to worship deities linked with fertility, water, and agriculture.

According to some researchers, the geoglyphs designate holy sites where gifts were made to appease gods and secure the community's well-being.

3. Water Culture and Irrigation:
Water Sources: Given the dry conditions, water was a valuable resource for the Nazca people. Some scholars

think the lines are connected to water sources or subsurface aquifers, thus acting as a hydrological map.

Aqueducts: The Nazca culture also built a vast network of aqueducts known as "puquios," demonstrating their excellent knowledge of water management. The wires might have been part of a larger scheme to harness and manage water.

Visit the Nazca Lines.
1. How To See the Lines:
Aerial Tours: The most common method of seeing the Nazca Lines is to take a small airplane trip. These flights provide a bird' s-eye perspective of the geoglyphs, enabling guests to fully appreciate their size and complexity.

Observation Towers: For those who prefer to remain on the ground, there are observation towers and overlooks along the Pan-American Highway. These provide limited yet spectacular views of several of the figurines.

2. Best time to visit:
Weather Considerations: The Nazca area is dry all year. However, the ideal time is winter (May to September) when temperatures are lower and visibility is often greater.

3. Preservation Efforts:
Conservation Challenges: Despite their isolated position, the Nazca Lines are threatened by human activities, including urban expansion, mining, and

vandalism. Natural erosion and climate change are additional potential hazards.

Protective Measures: The Peruvian government and international organizations have taken steps to save and preserve the geoglyphs. These include controlling planes, limiting access to vulnerable locations, and encouraging environmentally friendly tourist practices.

The Nazca Lines remain one of the world's most intriguing archeological riddles. These elaborate decorations' purpose and importance continue attracting scholars and tourists. Whether used as astronomical markers, ceremonial routes, or water management symbols, the lines provide an intriguing peek into the ancient Nazca civilization's creativity and cultural customs. Visiting the Nazca Lines is a historical adventure and a chance to reflect on the legacy of human innovation and adaptation in the face of adversity.

5.2 Paracas National Reserve: Wildlife and Scenic Beauty

Paracas National Reserve, situated on Peru's Pacific coast near Pisco, is a pristine coastal desert habitat known for its magnificent scenery, diversified animals, and rich cultural legacy. Established in 1975, the reserve covers 335,000 hectares and has a unique mix of desert, ocean, and marine environments. Paracas provides an exceptional natural experience, with cliffs, wind-sculpted dunes, quiet beaches, and teeming marine life. Here's a deeper look at the fauna and scenery of Paracas National Reserve.

Biodiversity and Wildlife
1. Marine life:
Rich Ecosystem: Paracas's seas off the coast form part of the Humboldt Current, one of the world's most prolific marine environments. This nutrient-rich stream supports a wide variety of aquatic creatures.

Birdlife: Paracas is a refuge for seabirds, with many species breeding on cliffs and rugged coasts. Visitors may see Humboldt penguins, Peruvian pelicans, cormorants, boobies, and the famous Inca tern.

Marine Mammals: The reserve also supports sea lions, fur seals, and dolphins. Boat cruises allow you to witness these species in their natural environment.

2. Desert Flora and Fauna:
Adaptations: Despite its dry temperature, the desert terrain of Paracas sustains a remarkable variety of plant

and animal species. Succulent plants like cactus and agaves flourish on sandy soils, while hardy shrubs and grasses populate the landscape.

Wildlife in the desert includes reptiles such as the Peruvian desert iguana and the South American sea snake, as well as small mammals such as the Peruvian and Andean foxes.

Scenic Beauty
1. Dramatic coastline:
Rock Formations: Paracas' rough coastline is defined by stunning cliffs, sea caves, and rock formations carved by wind and waves over millennia. The renowned Cathedral Rock is a natural arch feature that has become the reserve's emblem.

Paracas' beautiful beaches include silky, red-hued sands that contrast sharply with the deep blue waves of the Pacific Ocean. Playa Roja (Red Beach) is one of the reserve's most attractive and quiet places.

2. The Paracas Peninsula
Punta Arquillo: This picturesque overlook provides sweeping views of the coastline, allowing tourists to admire the rocky beauty of the Paracas Peninsula and the vast ocean beyond.

La Mina Beach is a peaceful cove flanked by high cliffs that is great for swimming, snorkeling, and picnics. It is just a short stroll from Punta Arquillo.

3. Ballestas Island:
The Ballestas Islands, situated close to the coast of Paracas, are a protected marine reserve rich in species.

Boat cruises to the islands provide close-up views of breeding seabirds, lively sea lions, and Humboldt penguin colonies.

Candelabra Geoglyph: On the way to the Ballestas Islands, travelers may see the enigmatic Candelabra Geoglyph, a large-scale figure engraved into the Paracas Peninsula's sandy slopes.

Conservation and Sustainable Tourism.
1. Preservation Efforts:
Protected Area: Paracas National Reserve is a UNESCO World Heritage Site and a Ramsar Wetland of International Importance, indicating its ecological value and biodiversity.
Conservation Initiatives: The Peruvian government, in partnership with local communities and conservation groups, is implementing steps to conserve the reserve's natural resources, including habitat restoration, wildlife monitoring, and sustainable tourism.

2. Sustainable Tourism Practices:
Visitor Education: Interpretive centers and guided excursions educate visitors about the reserve's environment, conservation issues, and cultural legacy.

Regulated Access: Visitor numbers and activities inside the reserve are tightly controlled to reduce environmental effects and protect fragile areas.

Community Involvement: Eco-tourism programs assist local communities by creating jobs, supporting local businesses, and promoting cultural interaction.

Paracas National Reserve demonstrates the beauty and durability of Peru's coastal desert ecosystems. From its varied animals and breathtaking scenery to its rich cultural legacy and dedication to conservation, Paracas provides tourists with a genuinely immersive and remarkable experience. Whether exploring the craggy coastline, witnessing seabird colonies, or sailing among the Ballestas Islands, visiting Paracas National Reserve takes you into the heart of Peru's natural treasures, where the desert meets the sea in a symphony of life and beauty.

5.3 The Oasis of Huacachina: Sandboarding and Adventure Sports

Nestled between towering dunes in the Peruvian desert, the Oasis of Huacachina is a bizarre and stunning desert oasis famed for its towering dunes, palm-fringed lagoon, and adrenaline-pumping adventure activities. Huacachina, located only a few kilometers west of Ica, offers tourists a unique combination of natural beauty and exhilarating outdoor activities, making it a must-see destination for both adventurers and nature lovers. Here's a deeper look at Huacachina's Oasis and the exciting adventure activities it offers.

Oasis Setting and Natural Beauty

1. Geological formation:
Natural Wonder: Huacachina is said to have evolved spontaneously thousands of years ago, nourished by subterranean aquifers that emerge surrounding the Oasis. Surrounded by massive dunes that reach up to 200 meters, the Oasis stands out against the arid environment.

Lush flora: Despite its dry surroundings, Huacachina is home to lush palm trees and other flora, providing a peaceful and green oasis in the desert.

2. Scenic Lagoon:

Huacachina's central feature is a tranquil lagoon whose emerald-green waters mirror the surrounding palm palms and dunes. Visitors may hire pedal boats or kayaks to explore the lagoon and enjoy the breathtaking views.

Sunset Views: Huacachina is especially lovely at sunset, when the departing light spreads a golden glow over the dunes, offering a captivating setting for photography and leisure.

Sandboarding and Adventure Sports

1. Sandboarding:

Thrilling Sport: Huacachina is well-known as one of the world's best sandboarding resorts. Sandboarding involves sliding down steep sand dunes on a specially-made board, similar to snowboarding on the sand.

Huacachina provides sandboarding adventures for all ability levels, whether you're an experienced adrenaline addict or a beginner searching for adventure. Beginners may choose modest slopes, while skilled riders can tackle steeper dunes for added excitement.

Local tour companies provide sandboarding training and equipment rental, guaranteeing that tourists may enjoy this exciting sport safely.

2. Dune Buggy Tours:

Off-Road Adventure: Dune buggy trips are a popular way to explore the enormous dunes surrounding Huacachina. These challenging off-road vehicles cross sandy terrain, providing riders an adrenaline-fueled adventure through the desert.

Spectacular Views: Dune buggy trips provide incredible panoramic views of the Oasis and adjacent desert scenery, creating memorable picture possibilities.

Sunset excursions: Sunset dune buggy excursions are very popular, as they enable guests to see the desert landscape bathed in the warm tones of the setting sun, producing a wonderful experience.

3. Sand skiing and sledding:
Alternative Activities: In addition to sandboarding, Huacachina tourists may attempt sand skiing or sand sledding. These sports, like their snow equivalents, require sliding down the dunes on skis or sleds, which provides a unique and thrilling experience.

Practical Tips for Visitors:

1. Sun Protection:
Sunscreen and Hats: The desert sun may be harsh, so wear sunscreen, sunglasses, and a wide-brimmed hat to avoid sunburn and dehydration.

Hydration: Bring lots of water to remain hydrated, mainly if you're doing outside activities in the heat.

2. Clothing and footwear:
Comfortable Clothing: Dress in lightweight, breathable clothing that gives sun protection and allows for freedom of movement. Avoid dark hues, which absorb heat.

Closed-Toe Shoes: Use sturdy, closed-toe shoes with adequate grip to travel sandy terrain securely.

3. Safety precautions:

Follow directions: Pay attention to directions from experienced guides and instructors, particularly while engaging in adventure sports such as sandboarding and dune buggy trips.

Stay on Designated Paths: Respect designated areas and paths to reduce environmental damage and prevent disorientation in the desert.

The Huacachina Oasis in the Peruvian desert offers tourists a spectacular combination of natural beauty and adrenaline-pumping adventure activities. It offers an unparalleled experience for tourists looking for thrill and adventure, from sandboarding down towering dunes to pedal boating around the picturesque lagoon. Whether you're a thrill-seeker searching for an adrenaline rush or a nature lover looking for breathtaking scenery, Huacachina offers something for everyone, making it a must-see location on any Peruvian expedition.

5.4 Arequipa, The White City and Its Charms

Arequipa, often known as "The White City," is a stunning combination of historical elegance, natural beauty, and cultural legacy set in the Andean foothills of southern Peru. Arequipa is renowned for its spectacular architecture, volcanic scenery, and rich culinary culture, providing tourists with a one-of-a-kind and memorable experience. Here's a deeper look at the attractions of Arequipa and why it's a must-see trip in Peru.

Colonial architecture.
1. Historic Center:
Arequipa's historic core, known for its well-preserved colonial architecture and white volcanic stone structures, has been named a UNESCO World Heritage Site. Strolling over its cobblestone streets is like returning to the colonial period.

La Plaza de Armas is the center of Arequipa. It is surrounded by prominent structures such as the magnificent Cathedral of Arequipa, which dates back to the 17th century, and the elaborate portals of neighboring buildings.

2. Santa Catalina Monastery

City Within a City: The Santa Catalina Monastery is a large convent complex that resembles a little city near Arequipa. Founded in 1579, this monastic enclave has colorful facades, tiny alleyways, and quiet courtyards that uniquely peek into Arequipa's colonial history.

Art and Architecture: The monastery is rich in art and architecture, including beautiful paintings, antique furniture, and religious relics that illuminate the lives of the nuns who lived there before.

Natural Wonders.
1. Volcanic landscapes:

Majestic Backdrop: Arequipa is flanked by towering volcanic peaks, including the renowned Misti, Chachani, and Pichu Pichu volcanoes, which dominate the cityscape. These snow-capped mountains provide a stunning backdrop to Arequipa's metropolitan setting and offer opportunities for outdoor activity.

Hiking & Trekking: Adventurers may join guided hikes and treks to explore the rugged terrain of the surrounding volcanoes, taking in spectacular panoramic vistas of the Andes along the route.

2. Colca Canyon:

Natural Wonder: A few hours' drive from Arequipa is Colca Canyon, one of the world's deepest canyons and a tribute to the region's geological variety. With its breathtaking views of terraced agriculture, soaring condors, and traditional Andean communities, Colca Canyon is a popular hiking, birding, and cultural immersion destination.

Hot Springs: After a day of exploring, travelers may relax in the canyon's natural hot springs, bathing in the healing waters while taking in the stunning surroundings.

Cultural Heritage
1. Gastronomy:
Culinary Delights: Arequipa is well-known for its diverse culinary traditions, which combine indigenous ingredients with Spanish, African, and Asian influences. Visitors from all over the globe enjoy local delicacies such as rocoto relleno (stuffed hot peppers), chupe de Camarones (shrimp soup), and adobo arequipeño (marinated pig stew).
Traditional picanterías, rustic restaurants providing substantial regional meals, are a must-visit for anyone wishing to experience the unique flavors of Arequipa.

2. Festivals and traditions:
Religious Celebrations: Arequipa is recognized for its lively festivals combining Catholic traditions with indigenous rites. The Feast of the Virgin of Chapi in May and the Feast of Our Lady of Mercy in September are two of the city's most notable religious celebrations, with colorful processions, music, and dancing.

Textile Art: Arequipa is well-known for its textile handicrafts, with artists creating beautifully woven fabrics utilizing ancient methods handed down through generations. Visitors may examine and buy these magnificent textiles at local markets and workshops around the city.

Arequipa, or the White City, captivates travelers with its timeless beauty, rich history, and dynamic culture. With its spectacular colonial architecture and volcanic scenery, as well as its gastronomic pleasures and vibrant festivals, Arequipa provides a multitude of experiences for tourists looking to immerse themselves in the spirit of Peru.

5.5 *Colca Canyon: Hiking and Condor Watching*

Colca Canyon, situated in the Arequipa area of southern Peru, is one of the world's deepest valleys and a natural marvel that appeals to explorers and nature lovers. Colca Canyon's stunning vistas, quaint settlements, and rich animals make it ideal for outdoor activities, including hiking and condor watching. Here's a deeper look at the hiking paths and the possibility of seeing condors in Colca Canyon.

Hiking Trails

1. Colca Canyon Trek:

The Colca Canyon walk is a multi-day hike through one of the world's most beautiful natural marvels. The walk includes a range of terrain, from moderate pathways around the canyon rim to arduous descents into the canyon.

The length of the journey varies based on the route and schedule. Most excursions span two to four days, giving plenty of time to explore the canyon's various landscapes and cultural attractions.

Highlights of the climb include panoramic views of the canyon's tiered slopes, lush agricultural terraces, and towering rock formations. The route traverses' traditional Andean villages, allowing tourists to connect with locals and learn about their cultures and ways of life.

2. Oasis of Sangalle

Descent to the Oasis: One of the most popular hiking sites in Colca Canyon is the Oasis of Sangalle, a green oasis tucked at the canyon's bottom. The route to the Oasis is steeped over brutal switchbacks, providing a challenging yet rewarding walking experience.

Accommodation: The Oasis of Sangalle has rustic lodges and campsites, offering tired hikers an excellent location to relax and recuperate among the canyon's natural splendor.

3. Cruz del Cóndor's Viewpoint:

Condor Viewing: The Cruz del Cóndor viewpoint is widely regarded as one of the best places in Colca Canyon to see the majestic Andean condor in flight. Visitors go to this spectacular overlook in the early morning to see these magnificent birds fly on thermal updrafts emerging from the canyon depths.

UniqueUnique Views: In addition to condor viewing, the Cruz del Cóndor viewpoint provides fantastic panoramic views of the canyon's cliffs, tumbling waterfalls, and meandering river below, making it a must-see for nature enthusiasts and photographers.

Condor Watching
1. Natural habitat:

The Andean condor is the world's most enormous flying bird, with a fantastic wingspan of up to 3 meters. Colca Canyon is an excellent environment for these famous birds, with deep ravines, thermal air currents, and abundant prey species that maintain a robust condor population.

Flight Patterns: Condors are most active early in the morning when thermal updrafts are highest. Visitors may observe these exquisite birds glide effortlessly above the canyon, catching thermals for food and mates.

2. Conservation efforts:

Conservation measures for the Andean condor and its habitat in Colca Canyon include habitat restoration, animal monitoring, and community-based conservation projects. Local governments collaborate closely with conservation groups and indigenous people to safeguard the long-term survival of this iconic species.

Environmental education programs and guided tours promote awareness about the value of maintaining the Andean condor and its role in the ecosystem. Visitors are urged to see condors correctly, with little disturbance, and in designated viewing places.

Practical Tips for Visitors:
1. Safety precautions:

Hydration: Carry plenty of water and remain hydrated, particularly for challenging excursions through the canyon's high-altitude environment.

Sun Protection: To protect oneself from the sun and UV radiation at high altitudes, use sunscreen, a wide-brimmed hat, and lightweight clothes.

Respect trail markers and remain on approved trails to reduce erosion and protect vulnerable ecosystems.

2. Condor Watching Etiquette:

Quiet observation: Avoid quick movements or loud sounds that may frighten or upset the condors.

Binoculars: Bring binoculars or a camera with a telephoto lens to improve your viewing experience and catch close-up shots of the condors in flight.

Leave No Trace: Take all rubbish with you and avoid feeding or approaching animals.

Colca Canyon provides an unparalleled chance for adventure enthusiasts to experience one of the world's most stunning natural settings while seeing the majestic Andean condor in its native environment. Whether starting on a multi-day walk through the canyon's challenging terrain or admiring condors flying above the Cruz del Cóndor viewpoint, travelers to Colca Canyon have an extraordinary experience that highlights the beauty and biodiversity of Peru's Andean highlands. Colca Canyon, with its rich cultural legacy, breathtaking views, and varied species, represents the spirit of adventure and discovery in the heart of South America.

Chapter Six: The Highlands and Lake Titicaca.

6.1 Puno and the shores of Lake Titicaca

Puno, a dynamic city in southern Peru, is on the banks of Lake Titicaca, the world's highest navigable lake. It is noted for its rich cultural legacy, traditional Andean traditions, and breathtaking natural scenery. Puno, as the entrance to the renowned floating islands of the Uros people and the holy islands of Taquile and Amantani, captivates tourists with its combination of history, culture, and natural beauty. Here's a journey to Puno and the lovely coastline of Lake Titicaca.

Cultural Heritage

1. Indigenous communities:
Uros Floating Islands: A journey to Lake Titicaca would only be complete with witnessing the Uros people's unique way of life, which consists solely of floating islands built of totara reeds. For millennia, the Uros lived on these artificial islands, which served as a refuge from outside dangers and a symbol of their strength and inventiveness.

Taquile Island is home to the Taquileños, an Indigenous Quechua-speaking population known for their complex handwoven fabrics and traditional weaving skills. The island also has terraced agricultural terrains. Visitors may explore the island's gorgeous paths, meet local artists, and learn about their cultural history.

2. Festivals and traditions:
Puno comes alive during the annual Candelaria Festival, one of the Andes's most significant and colourful events. This festive celebration in February offers exciting processions, music, dancing, and traditional costumes honouring Puno's patron saint, the Virgin of Candelaria.

Pachamama ceremonies: Indigenous ceremonies honouring Pachamama, or Mother Earth, are essential to Andean spiritual practice. Visitors to Puno may participate in rites and offerings to Pachamama, which are said to bring benefits and tranquillity to the town.

Natural beauty.

1. Lake Titicaca

Scenic splendour: Lake Titicaca's dazzling waters and snow-capped hills provide an incredible background for exploration and adventure. The lake's large surface area and crystalline waters sustain a complex aquatic environment, which includes Andean waterfowl, fish, and aquatic plants.

Boat Excursions: Guided boat cruises allow guests to explore the peaceful waters of Lake Titicaca, stopping by islands, peninsulas, and quiet coves along the route. Whether sailing to the Uros Islands, Taquile, or Amantani, each trip shows a different aspect of the lake's beauty and cultural importance.

2. Sillustani Burying Towers:

Sillustani, a pre-Inca burial site in Puno, is an archaeological gem set among rolling hills overlooking Lake Umayo. The site is known for its chullpas, or funeral towers, which were erected by the Indigenous Colla people to hold the remains of prominent members.

Cultural Significance: The chullpas of Sillustani are a witness to the spiritual beliefs and building skills of ancient Andean civilizations, providing tourists with an insight into the region's rich cultural history and funerary customs.

Local cuisine.

1. Puno Cuisine:

Andean tastes: Puno's culinary culture celebrates the unique flavours and ingredients of the Andean highlands, with dishes incorporating locally obtained delicacies such as quinoa, potatoes, fish, and alpaca meat. Traditional dishes include:

- Pachamanca (a beef and vegetable stew cooked underground).
- Trucha a la parrilla (grilled fish).
- Chuño (freeze-dried potatoes).

Lake Titicaca Cuisine: Puno's cuisine features freshwater fish from Lake Titicaca, mainly trout and kingfish. These specialties, along with Andean grains, veggies, and fragrant herbs, may be enjoyed at local restaurants and markets.

Puno, with its intriguing combination of cultural legacy, natural beauty, and spiritual traditions, provides tourists with a one-of-a-kind and immersive experience in the heart of the Andean highlands. Puno welcomes visitors to enjoy the beauty and mysticism of Lake Titicaca and its surrounding coasts, whether they explore the floating islands of the Uros people, hike the magnificent trails of Taquile Island, or attend the colorful celebrations of the Candelaria Festival. With its warm welcome, rich cultural tapestry, and spectacular panoramas, Puno exemplifies the Andean people's lasting spirit and eternal fascination with Peru's high-altitude beauties.

6.2 The Floating Island of Uros

The Floating Islands of Uros are a magnificent marvel of human ingenuity and adaptation. Nestled in the blue waters of Lake Titicaca, they are surrounded by towering hills and fresh Andean air. These man-made islands, fashioned completely of totora reeds, not only demonstrate the Indigenous Uros people's inventiveness but also serve as a living expression of their cultural history and way of life. Let us embark on a voyage to explore the beautiful world of the Floating Islands of Uros.

Origins and Construction

1. **Ancient Tradition:** The Uros have inhabited Lake Titicaca for millennia, extending back to pre-Columbian times. Faced with the problems of living in a harsh and unpredictable environment, they devised an intelligent solution: create floating islands out of totora reeds. This natural plant grows abundantly in the lake's shallows.

2. **Totora Reeds:** Totora reeds are the lifeblood of the Uros community, supplying construction materials for their islands, nourishment, and living. Reeds are collected, packed, and precisely piled to construct buoyant platforms capable of bearing the weight of whole towns.

Life on the islands

1. Stepping onto the Floating Islands of Uros seems like entering another world where time appears to stand still, and the ebb and flow of the lake governs the rhythm of life. The islands are home to a close-knit community of Uros families who live in traditional reed-thatched houses and follow ancient practices handed down through generations.

2. **Self-Sufficiency:** Despite their isolated position, the Uros people have established a self-sufficient lifestyle, depending on fishing, bird hunting, and handicrafts for food and money. Visitors visiting the islands may see traditional fishing practices, learn about reed weaving, and buy handcrafted gifts from local artisans.

Cultural Heritage
1. **Spiritual Connection:** Lake Titicaca is more than simply a body of water to the Uros people; it is a holy entity with spiritual meaning. They believe the lake is home to protecting spirits known as "khanates," who watch over their towns and safeguard their well-being.

2. **Preservation Efforts:** In recent years, the Uros have encountered many obstacles, including environmental deterioration, cultural assimilation, and economic hardship. However, attempts continue to maintain their distinctive way of life while protecting Lake Titicaca's endangered ecology. Sustainable tourism initiatives, community-based conservation programs, and cultural revitalization activities aim to preserve the Uros people's artistic legacy and livelihoods for future generations.

Visitor Experience
1. **Cultural Immersion:** Visiting the Floating Islands of Uros offers guests a unique chance to immerse themselves in the Andean highlands' rich cultural tapestry. Guided tours give insights into the Uros people's everyday lives, traditions, and rituals, enabling tourists to form personal connections with their hosts.

2. Boat trips from Puno provide easy access to the Floating Islands of Uros, enabling tourists to explore various islands and interact with the locals. Visitors may learn about the processes used to create the islands, engage in traditional rituals, and even take a trip in a "totora reed boat."

The Floating Islands of Uros are a living tribute to the Uros people's fortitude, resourcefulness, and cultural heritage—they demonstrate their creativity and flexibility in the face of hardship. As guests traverse the sparkling waters of Lake Titicaca to these distant and fascinating islands, they are met not only by magnificent natural beauty but also by the Uros community's warm hospitality and rich cultural traditions. In a world where modernity often trumps tradition, the Floating Islands of Uros remind us of the lasting spirit of indigenous civilizations and the ageless fascination of Peru's high-altitude marvels.

6.3 Taquile and Amantani Islands.

Taquile and Amantani Islands, located in the peaceful waters of Lake Titicaca, are two of Peru's most enchanting places. These islands, noted for their tranquil beauty, rich cultural legacy, and traditional way of life, provide tourists with an authentic experience deep in the Andean highlands. Each island has its distinct charm, history, and attractions, making them must-see destinations for visitors looking to see Peru's cultural and natural environments.

Taquile Island

1. **Cultural Heritage:**

Taquile Island is known for its colorful textile heritage, which UNESCO has designated a Masterpiece of the Oral and Intangible Heritage of Humanity. The men of Taquile are the primary weavers, producing complex fabrics depicting Andean iconography and daily life. Visitors may see these talented artists at work and buy lovely handcrafted textiles as souvenirs.

Community Structure: The island's community is based on a collective structure that values communal effort and mutual assistance. This ancient structure, known as "ayllu," is the foundation of social organization and ensures the well-being of all community members.

2. Scenic Beauty:

Terraced Agriculture: The Taquile landscape is characterized by terraced fields that have been farmed for generations. These terraces, mainly used to raise potatoes and quinoa, contribute to the island's stunning splendour while demonstrating the resourcefulness of ancient Andean farming processes.

Panoramic vistas: Hikers on Taquile Island are rewarded with stunning vistas of Lake Titicaca and its surrounding mountains. The island's highest point, about 4,050 meters above sea level, provides breathtaking views and is a favorite site for tourists to watch the sunset.

3. Cultural immersion:

Homestays: Staying with local families via homestay programs is one of the most authentic ways to explore the island's culture. Guests engage in everyday activities, eat together, and learn about their hosts' customs and traditions. This comprehensive event promotes cultural interchange and gives insight into the Taquileño way of life.

Taquile Island has various traditional festivals throughout the year, which include music, dancing, and rituals. These festivals, including the Fiesta de San Santiago and the Fiesta de San Pedro, allow tourists to experience and participate in the island's rich cultural traditions.

Amantani Island
1. Spiritual Significance:

Pachamama and Pachatata: Amantani Island is known for its spiritual importance, with two temples devoted to Pachamama (Mother Earth) and Pachatata (Father Earth).

These temples on the island's tallest summits serve as focal points for yearly rites and festivities. Visitors may climb to these temples to enjoy the tranquil ambience and breathtaking views of Lake Titicaca.

Traditional Rituals: Amantani residents undertake traditional rituals to commemorate the natural environment and their ancestors. These rituals, which include offerings and ceremonies, represent the community's strong spiritual connection to its surroundings.

2. Natural Beauty:
Terraced slopes: Like Taquile, Amantani Island has terraced slopes for agriculture. The island's good soil and suitable temperature enable the growth of a wide range of crops, including potatoes, maize, and barley.

Rich Scenery: The island's rich foliage, mixed with the turquoise waters of Lake Titicaca, produces a breathtaking scene ideal for trekking and exploration. Amantani's peacefulness makes it an ideal destination for those looking to escape the rush and bustle of city life.

3. Community Experience:
Welcoming Homestays: Amantani residents are recognized for their hospitality, inviting tourists into their homes and sharing their way of life. Homestay programs on the island provide a unique chance to live like a native, doing daily chores, preparing traditional meals, and learning about island culture.

Local Crafts: The islanders are accomplished craftsmen who produce beautiful handicrafts, including fabrics, pottery, and jewelry. These items are often sold at local markets, generating revenue for the community and allowing tourists to acquire unique, handcrafted keepsakes.

Practical information for visitors.
1. Getting there:
Boat Access: Taquile and Amantani Islands are accessible by boat from Puno. The boat excursion to Taquile takes around 2-3 hours, while the trip to Amantani takes over 4 hours. Many itineraries include visits to both islands, enabling guests to enjoy the distinct charms of each.

Travel Packages: Numerous travel companies in Puno offer guided trips to Taquile and Amantani, which frequently include boat transportation, lunches, and homestay lodgings. These trips are convenient ways to see the islands while obtaining insights from skilled local guides.

2. Accommodation:
Homestays: Staying with local families is the most popular lodging on both islands. Homestays facilitate cultural interaction while also benefiting the local economy. They typically cost $15 to $30 per night, including food.

Basic facilities: Although the islands provide basic facilities, visitors should be prepared for primitive living circumstances. Electricity is scarce, and there are no ATMs, so carry plenty of cash.

3. Health & Safety:
Altitude Considerations: Both islands are situated at high heights (about 4,000 meters above sea level), which might impact tourists who are unused to such elevations. It's critical to acclimate gradually, remain hydrated, and take it easy for the first several days.

Respectful Tourism: Visitors are urged to respect local customs and traditions, get permission before photographing individuals, and give back to the community by supporting local businesses and craftspeople.

Taquile and Amantani Islands provide a unique and rewarding experience for visitors interested in Lake Titicaca's cultural history and natural beauty.

6.4 Cultural Heritage and Local Traditions

Peru's cultural legacy is as varied and rich as its landscapes, including ancient civilizations, colonial influences, and millennia-old indigenous customs. From the breathtaking remains of Machu Picchu to the bustling festivals of Cusco, Peru's cultural tapestry is woven with a diverse range of traditions, rituals, and creative manifestations that represent the country's multicultural culture. Let's look at Peru's cultural legacy and local customs, which make it an appealing destination for tourists interested in history, art, and culture.

Ancient civilizations

1. Inca civilization:
Machu Picchu: As the Inca Empire's crown jewel, Machu Picchu exemplifies the Incas' architectural talent and spiritual legacy. This ancient fortress, hidden among the Andean peaks, is a UNESCO World Heritage Site and one of the New Seven Wonders of the World, attracting tourists worldwide to admire its mysterious beauty and technical wonders.

Sacred Valley: The Sacred Valley of the Incas, with its terraced fields, tiny communities, and archaeological monuments, provides insight into its agricultural, religious, and cultural traditions. Visitors may visit ancient sites like Ollantaytambo and Pisac to learn about the ancient civilization's agricultural practices, astrological expertise, and spiritual beliefs.

2. Pre-Columbian Culture:
Chavín de Huántar, an archaeological site in the Andean highlands, is known for its towering stone buildings and artistic sculptures from the Chavín culture (900-200 BCE). The location is said to have acted as a religious center and pilgrimage place, where shamans performed rituals to communicate with the divine.

Colonial Heritage
1. Spanish Influence:

Cusco: Once the capital of the Inca Empire, Cusco became the focal point of Spanish colonial power in Peru after Francisco Pizarro's conquest of the Incas in the 16th century. The city's historic core is a UNESCO World Heritage Site, known for its Spanish colonial buildings, baroque churches, and cobblestone streets.

Colonial architecture in Peru combines Spanish and Indigenous forms. Beautiful churches, monasteries, and houses are decorated with complex carvings, paintings, and gold leaf. Lima's Historic Center, with its vast plazas and colonial-era structures, is another reminder of Peru's colonial past.

Indigenous traditions
Andean Cosmic Vision:
Pachamama, often known as Mother Earth, is a divine goddess in Andean mythology who nurtures all life and represents nature's and humanity's interdependence. Rituals and gifts to Pachamama are essential to Andean spiritual practice since they celebrate seasonal cycles, soil fertility, and natural balance.

Inti Raymi, also known as the Festival of the Sun, is an ancient Inca celebration near the winter solstice to worship Inti, the Sun God. Today, the celebration is held yearly in Cusco with colorful processions, music, dance, and reenactments of Inca ceremonies, bringing thousands of people from all over the globe.

Folk art and craftsmanship
1. Textile Traditions:
Andean Weaving: Peru's textile culture goes back thousands of years, with indigenous people creating

beautiful fabrics utilizing skills handed down through generations. Textiles have vibrant colors, elaborate patterns, and meaningful motifs representing each community's cultural identity and worldview.

Marketplaces: Local markets, such as Pisac Market in the Sacred Valley and San Pedro Market in Cusco, provide a stunning assortment of handmade textiles, ceramics, jewelry, and other artisanal products. These allow tourists to support local craftsmen while also purchasing genuine souvenirs.

Music, dance, and festivals.
1. Traditional Music and Dance:
Huayno is a traditional Andean music genre known for its vibrant rhythms, musical instruments, and emotional lyrics. Instruments often used in Huayno concerts include the charango, quena, and zampogna.
Marinera: The marinara is a delicate and exquisite dance from Peru's coastal areas. It is distinguished by precise footwork, flowing moves, and colorful costumes. The dance is often performed at traditional festivals and cultural events, highlighting Peru's diverse history.

2. Festivals and celebrations:
Qoyllur Rit'i: The Qoyllur Rit'i festival, celebrated yearly in the Andean highlands, is a vivid celebration of Andean spirituality, cultural legacy, and biodiversity. The celebration incorporates colorful processions, traditional music, dance, and ceremonies commemorating the area's holy glaciers and mountains.

Virgen de la Candelaria: The Virgen de la Candelaria celebration in Puno in February is among the Andean area's most significant and colorful events. The celebration comprises elaborate processions, traditional dances, music, and religious services commemorating the Virgin of Candelaria, the patron saint of Puno.

Peru's cultural legacy and local customs are a monument to the country's rich history, unique cultural mosaic, and persistent spirit of innovation and perseverance. From the ancient civilizations of the Incas to the vivid festivals and creative manifestations of modern-day Peru, the country's cultural tapestry continues to inspire and attract people from across the globe.

6.5 Practical Tips for High-Altitude Travel

Travelling to high-altitude regions, such as the Andes Mountains or the Himalayas, maybe a fantastic experience, providing stunning vistas and unique cultural experiences. However, the decreased oxygen levels at high elevations might cause issues for passengers. Proper planning and awareness are vital to achieving a safe, pleasant, high-altitude trip. Here are some valuable suggestions for high-altitude travel:

1. **Understand Altitude Sickness.**
Symptoms:
Mild symptoms include headache, nausea, dizziness, tiredness, shortness of breath, and a lack of appetite.

Moderate to severe symptoms include a severe headache, vomiting, disorientation, loss of coordination, and trouble breathing. If these symptoms occur, seek medical attention immediately.

Types:
Acute Mountain Sickness (AMS) is common and typically mild but may worsen if not treated.
High-Altitude Cerebral Edema (HACE) is a severe and sometimes fatal condition that causes brain swelling.
High-Altitude Pulmonary Edema (HAPE) is a severe and life-threatening condition characterized by fluid buildup in the lungs.

2. Preparation Before Departure
Physical Fitness.
Get Fit: Being in excellent physical shape might help your body deal with high-altitude stress. Regular aerobic workouts like walking, jogging, and cycling may help you improve your overall fitness.
Consult a doctor, especially if you have pre-existing medical ailments or worries about high-altitude flying.

Medicine:
Acetazolamide (Diamox): Ask your doctor about taking acetazolamide, which may help prevent and alleviate symptoms of altitude sickness.

Other drugs: Bring drugs for common conditions, including headaches, upset stomach, and dehydration.

3. Acclimatisation Strategies

Gradual ascent:
Ascend gently: To give your body time to acclimate, rise gently. Spend a few days at intermediate altitudes before ascending to higher levels.

Rule of thumb: Once over 2,500 meters, increase your sleeping altitude by no more than 300-500 meters each day and take a rest day for every 1,000 meters gained.

Stay hydrated:
Drink plenty of fluids: High elevations may rapidly dehydrate you. Drink 3-4 liters of water every day and avoid alcohol and caffeine, which may lead to dehydration.

Eat Lightly:
Balanced Diet: Eat a high-carbohydrate, low-fat diet to stay energized and assist with acclimatization.

Small Meals: Eat smaller, more frequent meals to prevent overwhelming your digestive system.

4. **During Your Trip**
Listen to Your Body:
Monitor Symptoms: Be aware of how you feel. If you feel signs of altitude sickness, only climb farther once you have acclimatized.

Rest if Needed: Take pauses and allow your body to rest if you feel exhausted or ill.

Appropriate Clothing:

Layer up to adjust to fluctuating temperatures in high-altitude situations, which may be chilly and windy.

Sun Protection: To protect yourself against severe UV radiation at higher altitudes, use sunscreen, sunglasses, and a hat.

Prevent Overexertion:

Pace Yourself: Maintain a steady, comfortable pace. Avoid intense exertion, particularly in the first several days at high altitudes.

Rest Well: Make sure you receive adequate sleep so your body may recuperate and adapt.

5. Emergency Preparedness
Emergency Plan:

Know the Symptoms: Recognize the indications of severe altitude sickness and be ready to descend promptly if symptoms intensify.

Local Resources: Learn the locations of the closest medical facilities and emergency services.

Travel Insurance:

Coverage: Ensure your trip insurance covers high-altitude hiking and medical evacuation.

Keep a list of emergency contacts, such as local guides and medical professionals.

6. Cultural sensitivity
Respect local customs:

Respect the local customs and traditions. Engage with the local community in a respectful and culturally aware way. **Learn simple words:** Learning a few simple words in the local language will help you establish rapport and demonstrate respect.

Environmental responsibilities:
Leave No Trace: Adhere to the principles of responsible tourism by reducing your environmental effects. Dispose of rubbish responsibly and prevent disrupting natural ecosystems.

Support the Local Economy: Buying products and services from local merchants helps the local economy and community.

High-altitude travel may be a rewarding and fascinating experience, combining breathtaking natural beauty with rich cultural contacts. Understanding the hazards connected with high elevations and adopting the required measures will allow you to reduce the effect of altitude sickness while thoroughly enjoying your experience. Remember to properly prepare, climb carefully, remain hydrated, and listen to your body. With these practical recommendations, you'll be well-prepared to face the obstacles of high-altitude travel and make the most of your experience.

Chapter 7: The Northern Treasures

7.1 Trujillo: Colonial Charm, Archaeological Sites

Trujillo, situated on Peru's northern coast, seamlessly mixes colonial elegance with a rich archaeological past. Owing to its favorable environment, Trujillo is nicknamed the "City of Eternal Spring." It provides tourists a unique blend of historical architecture, lively cultural events, and proximity to some of Peru's most important pre-Columbian archaeological sites. Here's a comprehensive look at what makes Trujillo a must-see location.

Colonial Charm
1. Historic Center:
Plaza de Armas: The hub of Trujillo's historic district, Plaza de Armas is surrounded by colorful colonial buildings and essential structures, including the Trujillo Cathedral, which dates from the 17th century. The plaza is a popular meeting location, particularly in the evening.

Trujillo church: This beautiful church, with its yellow front and rich interior, is an excellent example of colonial architecture. It has a museum that displays religious relics and artwork.

Colonial houses: The city has numerous well-preserved colonial houses, like Casa Urquiaga and Casa Ganoza

Chopitea, that provide insight into the lavish lifestyle of Trujillo's colonial aristocracy. These residences have beautiful courtyards, vintage furnishings, and detailed woodwork.

2. Cultural vibrancy:

Marinera Dance: Trujillo is famed for its Marinera, a classic Peruvian dance with delicate moves and gorgeous costumes. The annual Marinera Festival in January draws dancers and onlookers from around the nation and beyond the globe.

Festivals & Events: In addition to the Marinera Festival, Trujillo holds various cultural events throughout the year, including the International Spring Festival, which incorporates parades, flower exhibitions, and beauty competitions.

Archaeological sites
1. Chan Chan :

Chan Chan, the world's biggest adobe city, served as the capital of the Chimu civilization. This UNESCO World Heritage Site spans around 20 square kilometres and comprises nine walled citadels, each with temples, plazas, and houses.

Complex Carvings: The walls of Chan Chan are covered with complex carvings and friezes showing fish, birds, and geometric patterns, indicating the Chimu's affinity for the sea and creative talent.

Visitor Experience: The Tschudi Complex is one of the best-preserved areas exposed to the public. Visitors may visit the ceremonial plazas, royal apartments, and burial platforms to learn more about Chimu culture and civilization.

2. Huaca de la Luna, Huaca del Sol:
Moche Pyramids: The Moche culture built two massive pyramids. The largest of the two, the Huaca del Sol, was used mainly for administrative purposes, and the Huaca de la Luna was a religious and ceremonial centre.

Stunning paintings: The paintings of the Huaca de la Luna, which are in excellent condition, represent Moche deities, warriors, and mythical settings. These vivid paintings detail Moche's beliefs, ceremonies, and everyday life.

Archaeological Insights: Excavations at these sites have yielded various items, including pottery, tools, and human remains, which provide a better knowledge of Moche society. Guided tours offer guests in-depth explanations of the importance and history of these outstanding monuments.

3. El brujo:
El Brujo is another notable Moche site, noted for its massive adobe pyramid, the Huaca Cao Viejo.
The finding of the mummy of the Lady of Cao, a high-ranking female chieftain, was one of El Brujo's most noteworthy discoveries. The mummy, dressed with ornate tattoos and jewelry, reveals the position of women in Moche culture.

The site has a museum showcasing objects discovered during excavations, including pottery, textiles, and the bones of the Lady of Cao. Visitors may learn about the Moche civilization's social organization, religious beliefs, and artistic accomplishments.

Practical information.
1. Getting there:
Trujillo is connected by direct flights from Lima and other important Peruvian cities. Capitán FAP Carlos Martínez de Pinillos International Airport is around 10 kilometers from the city center.

Ground Transportation: Trujillo is well-connected by bus to other regions of Peru. The city's bus station provides service to and from Lima, Chiclayo, and other regional locations.

2. Accommodation:
Trujillo has many lodging alternatives, from luxury hotels and boutique inns to low-cost hostels and guesthouses. Staying in the historic centre provides easy access to key attractions.
Some popular hotels are Costa del Sol Wyndham Trujillo, Hotel El Gran Marqués, and Casa Andina Standard Trujillo Plaza.

3. Safety and Tips:
Trujillo is typically safe for travelers; however, they should take conventional measures, such as avoiding secluded places at night, keeping valuables secure, and utilizing recognized transportation services.

When visiting archaeological sites and religious monuments, dress modestly and follow local norms. Photography may be prohibited in some situations, so always get permission before taking pictures.

Trujillo impresses us as a city that combines colonial charm with historic heritage. Visitors to Trujillo are treated to a fascinating voyage through time as they meander through the cobblestone alleyways of its old center, admire the majestic adobe architecture of Chan Chan, or explore the beautiful paintings of the Huaca de la Luna. The city's thriving cultural scene, friendly residents, and diverse archaeological riches make it a must-see for anyone who knows Peru's history better.

7.2 Chiclayo: The Lord of Sipán and the Túcume Pyramids

In northern Peru, Chiclayo is a settlement that provides a gateway to some of the most important archaeological sites of the ancient Moche and Lambayeque civilizations. Due to its friendly residents, Chiclayo is known as the "City of Friendship" and offers a diverse range of cultural legacy, historical interest, and breathtaking scenery. The Royal Tombs of Sipán and Túcume Pyramids near Chiclayo provide fascinating insights into Peru's pre-Columbian history.

The Lord of Sipán
1. **Discovery and Significance:**
Tomb Discovery: In 1987, Peruvian archaeologist Walter Alva uncovered the tomb of the Lord of Sipán, one of the

twentieth century's most important archaeological discoveries. This tomb, found in the Huaca Rajada site, held the remains of a Moche monarch, together with an astonishing variety of gold, silver, and copper items, as well as pottery vessels, textiles, and other tributes.

Historical significance: The discovery of the Lord of Sipán's tomb revealed significant information about the Moche culture, which existed between 100 and 700 AD. The abundance of burial gifts reflected the Lord's great rank and the intricacy of Moche society and its hierarchical system.

2. Royal Tombs Museum:

Exhibit Highlights: The Royal Tombs Museum of Sipán, situated in the village of Lambayeque near Chiclayo, was founded to hold and show the magnificent objects discovered in the tomb. The museum is meant to seem like a Moche tomb, providing visitors with a one-of-a-kind, immersive experience.

Artefacts on Display: The museum's collection contains the Lord of Sipán's exquisite regalia, including gold headdresses, necklaces, earspools, and other ceremonial objects. The meticulous quality of these items demonstrates the Moche's sophisticated metallurgical abilities.

Educational Insights: The museum's displays provide thorough information on Moche culture, religion, and everyday life, as well as the importance of the Sipán find.

Visitors may learn about the objects' background and relevance via interactive exhibits and guided tours.

3. Visit Huaca Rajada:

Archaeological Site: The tomb was found at the Huaca Rajada site, about 35 kilometers east of Chiclayo. Visitors may visit the excavation site and view the burial platforms where the Lord of Sipán and other prominent figures were buried.

Site Museum: A tiny on-site museum provides extra context for the excavations and showcases some of the objects discovered at Huaca Rajadas. This adds to the experience of visiting the Royal Tombs Museum and offers a thorough knowledge of the findings.

Túcume Pyramids
1. Archaeological Complex:

The Túcume Pyramids, also known as the Valley of the Pyramids, is a vast archaeological complex that includes 26 large pyramids and several lesser constructions. The Lambayeque (Sicán) culture created these pyramids after the Moche, and the Chimú and Inca civilizations subsequently utilized them.

Huaca Larga is the complex's greatest feature, a gigantic adobe pyramid over 700 meters in length. This pyramid functioned as a ceremonial and administrative center and provided panoramic views of the surrounding region.

2. Historical Context:

Lambayeque Culture: The Lambayeque culture, which existed between 750 and 1375 AD, was notable for its outstanding architectural marvels and metallurgical breakthroughs. The Túcume Pyramids showcase their engineering talents and religious rituals.

The Chimú and Inca civilizations inhabited the site and expanded the old constructions, demonstrating cultural continuity. This continuity emphasizes the site's historical importance and position as a cultural and religious center in northern Peru.

3. Site Museum and Visitors' Experience:

The Túcume Museum explores the history and importance of the pyramids. Exhibits include ceramics, tools, textiles, and educational exhibits concerning the site's excavation and conservation activities.

Guided tours provide tourists with thorough explanations of the pyramids' construction, function, and cultural significance. Local guides offer intriguing anecdotes about the Lambayeque, Chimú, and Inca civilizations.

Exploration & Hiking: Visitors may explore the site by following well-marked routes to several pyramids and views. The trek up to Huaca Larga provides a beautiful perspective of the ancient complex and adjacent valley.

Practical information for visitors.
1. Getting there:

Chiclayo is well-connected by air and land. Chiclayo's Capitán FAP José A. Quiñones International Airport receives daily flights from Lima and other important

150

cities. Buses travel regularly between Chiclayo and other parts of Peru.

Local travel options include cabs or organized trips from Chiclayo to Huaca Rajada, Lambayeque, and the Túcume Pyramids. Many tour companies combine visits to these places to provide convenient and educational travel alternatives.

2. Accommodation:

Chiclayo has various housing alternatives to suit different budgets and interests. Visitors may find acceptable housing alternatives near key sites, ranging from luxury hotels to budget-friendly hostels.

Some prominent hotels are Casa Andina Select Chiclayo, Sunec Hotel, and Costa del Sol Wyndham Chiclayo.

3. Tip for Visitors:

Climate and Clothing: The weather in Chiclayo is warm all year. Wear light, breezy clothes, sunscreen, and a hat for daytime outings. Evenings might be chilly, so a light jacket may be beneficial.

Respect for Sites: When visiting archaeological sites, refrain from touching or climbing on buildings to help preserve them. Follow the directions of site administrators and tour guides to ensure a polite and informed visit.

Chiclayo is a city that appeals to both historians and cultural explorers. The Lord of Sipán and Túcume Pyramids provide insight into Peru's ancient civilizations, highlighting the Moche and Lambayeque cultures' creativity, artistry, and spirituality. Chiclayo offers a rich tapestry of history and legacy, from the Royal Tombs Museum to the Túcume pyramids.

7.3 Chachapoyas and the Kuelap Fortress.

Chachapoyas, the Amazonas region's capital in northern Peru, is a lovely town famed for colonial architecture and lush surroundings. It is also close to one of Peru's most remarkable archaeological monuments, the Kuelap Fortress. Kuelap, sometimes known as the "Machu Picchu of the North," is a breathtaking pre-Inca structure that provides insight into the ancient Chachapoya culture. The natural beauty, historical intrigue, and cultural diversity make Chachapoyas and Kuelap a must-see destination for adventurous travellers.

Chachapoyas: The Gateway to History and Nature.
1. **Colonial Charm:**
Historical Center: Chachapoyas' historic center is a charming district with tiny lanes, whitewashed houses, and wooden balconies covered with colorful flowers. The Plaza de Armas is the town's hub, surrounded by landmarks like the Cathedral of St. John the Baptist.

Friendly Atmosphere: Known as the "Warriors of the Clouds", owing to the Chachapoya people's past, the town is now tranquil and hospitable, with a strong feeling of community and tradition.

2. **Natural Attractions:**

Gocta Waterfall: One of the world's highest waterfalls, Gocta is a spectacular two-tiered cascade that plunges 771 meters into the lush forest. It may be accessed by a magnificent stroll through the jungle, with the opportunity to see various flora and wildlife along the route.

The Chachapoya employed anthropomorphic sarcophagi on cliff ledges to bury their aristocracy, known as Karajía sarcophagi. The climb to the location offers breathtaking views of the surrounding area.

The Kuelap Fortress
1. Historical Background:

Chachapoya Civilization: The Chachapoya people, known as the "Cloud Warriors," erected Kuelap in the sixth century AD. This civilization flourished until the 16th century when the Incas subjugated it just before the arrival of the Spanish.

Kuelap is said to have functioned as a fortified city, ceremonial centre, and shelter for the Chachapoya nobility. Its strategic placement atop a mountain range afforded natural protection against attackers.

2. Architectural marvels:

Gigantic Walls: The stronghold is encircled by enormous stone walls that extend up to 20 meters high, with just three small openings. These walls were built with limestone stones, demonstrating the Chachapoya's great engineering talents.

Interior constructions: The castle has around 400 circular stone constructions on various levels. These structures comprise residential homes, ceremonial platforms, and storage areas. Some buildings include detailed carvings and ornamental friezes.

3. Unique Features:
El Tintero is one of Kuelap's most remarkable monuments. It is a conical tower that is said to have had a ceremonial or astronomical role, but archaeologists continue to question its function.

Feline and snake designs: Some structures' stone walls are carved with decorative feline and snake designs, symbolizing the Chachapoya's spiritual beliefs and creative expression.

4. Visitor Experience:
Cable Car Ride: Introducing a new cable car system has simplified getting to Kuelap considerably. The cable car trip provides fantastic views of the surrounding valleys and mountains, which enhances the whole experience.

Guided Tours: Knowledgeable guides conduct in-depth tours of the site, discussing the history, architecture, and importance of Kuelap. These trips provide vital insights and deepen visitors' awareness of the old Chachapoya culture.

Practical information for visitors.
1. Getting there:
Chachapoyas is accessible by bus from major cities such as Lima, Chiclayo, and Tarapoto. The town also has a tiny airport; however, airline options are limited. Many people

choose the picturesque bus route from Chiclayo, which takes around 10 hours.

Kuelap may be reached from Chachapoyas by road or cable car. The journey to the cable car station in Nuevo Tingo takes around an hour, followed by a 20-minute cable car trip and a short climb to the destination.

2. Accommodation:

Chachapoyas has many lodging alternatives, including low-cost hostels, mid-range hotels, and lovely guesthouses. Staying in town allows you easy access to Kuelap and other surrounding attractions.

Casa Hacienda Achamaqui, Gocta Andes Lodge, and La Xalca Hotel are popular lodging options.

3. Tip for Visitors:

The best time to visit Kuelap and Chachapoyas is during the dry season, which runs from April to November. The weather is more conducive to outdoor sports and trekking.

Physical Preparation: Visiting Kuelap requires trekking and walking, so bring comfortable shoes and be prepared for moderate physical exercise. The altitude (about 3,000 meters) may also be challenging, so take it slowly and remain hydrated.

Local Guides: Hiring a local guide may improve your stay by giving essential background and anecdotes that bring Kuelap's past alive.

Chachapoyas and the Kuelap Fortress provide an astonishing glimpse into Peru's lesser-known but equally fascinating historical and cultural history. The colonial elegance of Chachapoyas town and the awe-inspiring stone walls of Kuelap provide tourists with a rich tapestry of experiences that demonstrate the Chachapoya civilization's resourcefulness and perseverance.

7.4 Northern Beaches (Mancora and Piura)

Peru's northern coast is home to some of the country's most beautiful and bustling beach towns, including Mancora and Piura. These regions include sun-kissed beaches, fantastic surfing conditions, good seafood, and a laid-back ambience that draws local and foreign visitors. Mancora and Piura provide something for everyone, whether you want to relax by the beach or go on an adventure.

Mancora; Peru's premier beach destination.

Beach Town Vibes: Mancora is a tiny beach town in the Piura area known for its gorgeous sandy beaches, mild weather all year, and vibrant but relaxing vibe. It has transformed from a modest fishing community to a significant tourist destination.

Beach Activities:

Surfing and kite surfing: Mancora is well-known for its outstanding surfing conditions, with steady waves suitable for novice and expert surfers. Kite surfing is extremely popular owing to the high winds along the shore.

156

Swimming and Sunbathing: The main beach, Playa Mancora, has crystal-clear seas and smooth sand ideal for swimming and sunbathing. The beach is bordered with palm trees and beach bars, providing a lovely atmosphere.

Whale watching: From August to October, humpback whales may be observed moving along the shore. Boat cruises are provided for whale viewing, allowing you to see these majestic animals up close.

3. Nightlife & Dining:
Beach Bars and Clubs: Mancora has a thriving nightlife, with several beach bars and clubs open late. Loki Hostel and the well-known Surfer's Bar are popular places to visit.

Seafood Delights: The town is known for its fresh seafood. Restaurants provide great ceviche, grilled fish, and other Peruvian favourites. Notable restaurants include La Sirena d'Juan and Tao Asian Fusion.

4. Accommodation:
Mancora has diverse lodging alternatives, from inexpensive hostels to luxurious beachside resorts. Many sites have beautiful ocean views and direct beach access. Popular lodging options include DCO Suites, Mancora Marina Hotel, and Selina Mancora.

Piura: Gateway to the Northern Beaches.
Historical significance: Francisco Pizarro created Piura, one of Peru's oldest towns, in 1532. It is a gateway to the

northern beaches, blending historic elegance and contemporary conveniences.

Cultural Attractions: Piura has various cultural attractions, including the Cathedral of Piura, the Plaza de Armas, and the Miguel Grau Museum, honoring the legendary Peruvian naval hero.

2. Nearby beaches:

Colán Beach, located 60 kilometers from Piura, is famed for its calm waves and extensive sandy shoreline. It is a quieter alternative to Mancora and is ideal for leisure and family trips.

Vichayito Beach, located near Mancora, has a more serene atmosphere and fewer tourists. It's great for people seeking tranquil beach days and breathtaking sunsets.

3. Cuisine Scene:

Traditional food: Piura is famous for its particular regional food. Local cuisine includes Seco de Chavelo, a substantial pork stew, and Algarrobina, a sweet drink from carob tree pods.

Notable restaurants in Piura include El Chalan del Norte, which serves traditional Peruvian meals, and Tayanti, which combines local and foreign tastes.

4. Accommodation:

Piura offers various lodging alternatives, ranging from boutique hotels to comfortable inns. Staying in Piura provides convenient access to the city's cultural attractions and adjacent beaches.

Popular hotels in Piura include Casa Andina Premium Piura, Hotel Gran Palma, and Costa del Sol Wyndham Piura.

Practical information for visitors.
1. Getting there:
Both Mancora and Piura are accessible by plane. Mancora's closest airport is Talara Airport, approximately 80 kilometres away, with daily flights from Lima. Piura has its airport, Capitán FAP Guillermo Concha Iberico International Airport, which receives regular flights from major Peruvian cities.

Ground Transportation: Traveling from Piura to Mancora takes two hours. Buses and taxis are widely accessible, making getting between the two locations simple.

2. Best time to visit:
Year-Round Destination: Mancora and Piura are open year-round; however, the peak season runs from December to March, when the weather is hottest and driest. This time is great for beach activities and enjoying the seaside atmosphere.

3. Tip for Visitors:
Beach essentials include sunscreen, caps, and sunglasses. The sun may be harsh, particularly during noon.

Local customs: Peruvians are kind and welcoming. Learning simple Spanish words can improve your travel experience and interactions with locals.

The northern beaches of Mancora and Piura provide an intriguing blend of natural beauty, cultural richness, and recreational opportunities. Mancora's dynamic beach scene and superb surfing conditions make it a popular option for those looking for excitement and adventure. Piura provides a more relaxed experience with historical sights and neighboring tranquil beaches. Together, these sites offer the ideal beach escape that highlights the finest of Peru's northern coastline.

7.5 Adventure Activities: Surfing, Hiking, and Wildlife Watching.

Peru's landscapes provide various adventure activities for adrenaline seekers and nature lovers alike. Whether surfing the waves on the northern beaches, walking through the Andean mountains, or witnessing unique species in the Amazon jungle, Peru offers endless options for remarkable experiences.

Surfing
1. **Northern beaches include Mancora and Piura.**
Mancora: Mancora is Peru's top surfing location, with consistent waves year-round suitable for surfers of all skill levels. The major beach, Playa Mancora, has lengthy, left-hand point breakers ideal for both novice and expert surfers. Several surf schools and rental companies provide courses and equipment to beginners.

Other beaches in the Piura area, including Lobitos and Cabo Blanco, are well-known for their exceptional surf conditions. Lobitos is recognized for its solid and hollow waves, while Cabo Blanco is known for its perfect barrels, which draw elite surfers from all over the globe.

2. Central and southern coasts:
Punta Hermosa: Located near Lima, Punta Hermosa is another renowned surfing destination with waves perfect for all ability levels. It's an excellent choice for a fast-surfing excursion from the city.

Huanchaco: Huanchaco, in Trujillo, is a surfing hotspot and a cultural site where local fishermen have utilized traditional reed boats known as "caballitos de totora" for decades. The beach boasts steady waves and a relaxed ambience, making it perfect for surfers who want to enjoy sport and culture.

Hiking
1. Inca Trail to Machu Picchu:
Classic Inca Trail: This world-famous walk takes four days through the Sacred Valley and ends in a spectacular dawn vista of Machu Picchu. The path travels through varied ecosystems, old ruins, and breathtaking mountain views, providing a challenging yet rewarding experience.

Alternative Routes: For those looking for less congested pathways, alternative treks such as the Salkantay Trail and the Lares Trek provide unique views of the Andean nature while still getting to Machu Picchu. These routes offer equally stunning vistas and the opportunity to visit distant settlements and unspoiled settings.

2. Colca Canyon:

Deep Canyon Hikes: Colca Canyon is one of the deepest canyons, with various hiking paths suitable for all fitness levels. Treks generally entail descending into the canyon, crossing the Colca River, and climbing again, with the possibility of observing Andean condors and traditional terraced agriculture en route.

Condor Watching: One of the highlights of trekking in Colca Canyon is the beautiful Andean condor. Viewpoints like Cruz del Condor provide excellent opportunities to view these fantastic birds flying on thermal currents.

3. Huascarán National Park:

Cordillera Blanca: Huascarán National Park, home to the world's highest tropical mountain range, offers some of the greatest high-altitude hiking. Trails like the Santa Cruz Trek offer breathtaking vistas of snow-capped peaks, turquoise lakes, and rich flora and fauna.

Climbing peaks such as Huascarán or Alpamayo is an exciting task for skilled mountaineers. These climbs demand technical abilities and acclimatization, but climbers are rewarded with breathtaking views and a feeling of accomplishment.

Wildlife Watching
1. The Amazon Rainforest

Iquitos and Puerto Maldonado are gateway towns to some of the world's most biodiverse areas. Guided trips into the Amazon basin allow you to observe various species, including monkeys, sloths, colorful birds, and rare insects. Tambopata National Reserve is well-known for its abundant biodiversity. Visitors may hike forest paths, boat along rivers, and stay in eco-lodges that provide luxurious amenities while reducing environmental effects. Highlights include viewing gigantic river otters, macaws, and caimans.

2. Paracas National Reserve:

Aquatic Wildlife: Paracas National Reserve, on Peru's southern coast, is a sanctuary for marine life. During boat cruises to the Ballestas Islands, guests may witness sea lion colonies, Humboldt penguins, and a variety of seabirds. The reserve's coastline settings also provide breathtaking vistas and chances for kayaking and snorkeling.

Flamingo Watching: The reserve's wetlands are home to enormous flocks of flamingos that may be observed foraging in shallow waters. These gorgeous birds bring a pop of colour to an already stunning landscape.

3. Manu National Park:

Pristine Rainforest: Manu National Park, a UNESCO World Heritage site, is one of the most biodiverse places on Earth. Multi-day trips investigate the park's unspoiled jungle, where visitors may observe a wide range of wildlife, such as jaguars, gigantic otters, and an astounding diversity of birds and insects.

Cultural Encounters: Along with animals, Manu National Park is home to Indigenous cultures. Some trips visit these villages respectfully and instructively, giving insights into their traditional ways of life and strong relationships to the forest.

Practical Tips for Adventure Activities
1. Preparing to Surf:
Equipment: If you don't have your gear, many beaches rent surfboards, wetsuits, and other necessities. You should also bring sunscreen, a hat, and a drink to remain hydrated.

Lessons: Beginners should take lessons from licensed instructors to understand the fundamentals and be safe in the water.

2. Preparing to Hike:
Acclimatization: Many of Peru's trekking spots are at high elevations. Allow yourself a few days of acclimatization before climbing to avoid altitude sickness. Staying hydrated and avoiding intense activities in the beginning may assist.

Gear: Hiking boots, layered clothes, a hat, and a solid backpack are required. For logistical and safety reasons, consider hiring a guide or joining a tour group for multi-day excursions.

3. Preparing for Wildlife Watching:
Respect Wildlife: Keep a safe distance from animals and don't disrupt their natural activity. Follow the instructions supplied by your advisors and the local authorities.

Eco-Friendly Practices: Select eco-friendly trips that promote conservation and help local communities. Bring biodegradable toiletries and use less plastic to limit your environmental effects.

Peru's natural richness provides limitless options for adventure, whether you're surfing waves on its northern beaches, climbing through the gorgeous Andes, or discovering the Amazon rainforest's abundant wildlife. Each activity offers both thrills and excitement and a greater understanding of the country's distinct landscapes and customs. Whether a seasoned adventurer or a curious visitor, Peru's surfing, hiking, and wildlife-viewing adventures will leave you with unique memories and deep respect for this magnificent nation.

Made in United States
Orlando, FL
25 November 2024

54483372R00095